English for
Football

EXPRESS SERIES

Alan Redmond &
Sean Warren

OXFORD
UNIVERSITY PRESS

OXFORD
UNIVERSITY PRESS

Great Clarendon Street, Oxford, OX2 6DP, United Kingdom

Oxford University Press is a department of the University of Oxford.
It furthers the University's objective of excellence in research, scholarship,
and education by publishing worldwide. Oxford is a registered trade
mark of Oxford University Press in the UK and in certain other countries

ISBN: 978 0 19 457972 8

Printed in China

This book is printed on paper from certified and well-managed sources

ACKNOWLEDGEMENTS

*The authors and publisher are grateful to those who have given permission to reproduce
the following extracts and adaptations of copyright material:* p.5 Foreword by Sir
Alex Ferguson. Reproduced by permission; p.11 Interview with Lucas Leiva.
Reproduced by permission; p.19 Interview with Fabio and Rafael da Silva.
Reproduced by permission; p.27 Interview with Paul Pogba. Reproduced by
permission; p.33 Interview with Josep Segura. Reproduced by permission;
p.37 Interview with Luis Suàrez. Reproduced by permission; p.40 Interview
with Ben Amos. Reproduced by permission; p.45 Interview with David de
Gea. Reproduced by permission; p.49 Interview with Frank McParland.
Reproduced by permission; p.53 Interview with Javier Hernández.
Reproduced by permission; p.59 Interview with Eric Steele. Reproduced by
permission; p.61 Interview with Park Ji-Sung. Reproduced by permission.

*The publisher would like to thank the following for their kind permission to reproduce
photographs:* Sir Alex Ferguson CBE p.5; Alamy Images pp.16 (teenage boy
with football/i love images), 20 (man standing in the park/i love images/
Fitness), 22 (footballer in front of goal/Phovoir), 44 (Boy smiling/i love images),
47 (Two men talking/PhotoAlto sas), 68 (Male student/Chris Rout), 72 (Whistle/
Mode/Richard Gleed), 73 (red card/Rob Wilkinson), 73 (World cup/Nikreates);
Corbis pp.6 (Wayne Rooney/Simon Stacpoole), 6 (EFA Champions League
Final 2011/Joe Toth), 6 (UEFA Champions League Semifinal/Christian Liewig),
6 (FIFA World Cup 2010 Finals/Andres Kudacki), 7 (Soccer – UEFA Europa
League – Group A/Matt West), 7 (2010 FIFA World Cup South Africa – Group
F/Catherine Ivill), 10 (Barclays Premier League – Stoke City v Chelsea/
Catherine Ivill), 10 (Brazil vs Peru/ANTONIO LACERDA), 10 (International
Friendly/Matthew Ashton), 10 (Luis Manuel Rubiales/F. ALVARADO), 10 (Theo
Walcott of Arsenal/Catherine Ivill/AMA), 10 (Linesman Referee Holding Flag/
Turba), 13 (International Friendly – Brazil v Ghana/Catherine Ivill), 17 (Soccer
player standing with ball/Ocean), 18 (Chelsea v West Bromwich Albion/
Matthew Ashton), 22 (Man Posing with Soccer Ball/Ocean/Corbis), 22 (Portrait
of a footballer/mage Source), 22 (CAF African Cup of Nations Quarter finals/
Ben Radford), 22 (International Friendly – England v Spain/BPI), 23 (Ryan Giggs/
Matthew Ashton), 23 (Euro 2008 Qualification/Christian Liewig), 23 (FIFA
World Cup Spain vs. Portugal/Ben Queenborough), 30 (Liverpool vs. Stoke
City/Phil Oldham), 30 (Ronaldo shoots on goal/Alberto Martin), 30 (Andorra
vs. England/Matthew Ashton), 34 (Portrait of a teenage boy/Big Cheese Photo),
38 (Iker Casillas 2006/PCN), 38 (UEFA Champions League/Visionhaus),
40 (England U21 v Azerbaijan/Marc Atkins), 43 (Aston Villa vs. Liverpool/
Matthew Ashton), 48 (English Division One – Manchester United/Colorsport),
54 (Barcelona vs Arsenal FC/ANDREU DALMAU), 65 (FIFA World Cup 1974
Finals/Rolf Kosecki), 72 (International Friendly – England v Spain/BPI),
72 (Wayne Rooney/Simon Stacpoole), 73 (Linesman Referee Holding Flag/

Turba), 73 (Euro 2008 Qualification/Christian Liewig); Getty Images pp
(Barcelona's Argentinian forward Lionel M/JOSE JORDAN), 6 (VfB Stuttgart v
FC Bayern/Alexander Hassenstein), 10 (Portrait of smiling man/
amanaimagesRF), 11 (Cristiano Ronaldo/Angel Martinez), 12 (Football boots/
Hugh Threlfall), 14 (Thierry Henry/DANIEL GARCIA/AFP), 14 (John Terry/IAN
KINGTON), 15 (Boy holding football/Rubberball/Alan Bailey), 18 (England v
Sweden – International Friendly/Mike Hewitt), 19 (French Lilian Thuram/
scoresPASCAL GEORGE/AFP), 25 (Footballer/StockImage), 28 (Two men in
changing room in discussion/Adri Berger), 29 (Manchester United v West
Bromwich Albion/Michael Regan), 30 (Manchester United v Manchester/
Alex Livesey), 30 (goalkeeper Raul Fernandez dives/OMAR TORRES),
31 (Cameroon v Colombia/Henri Szwarc), 33 (Pele/Hulton Archive), 33 (Diego
Maradona/Bob Thomas), 36 (Sports coach instructing boys/Bob Thomas),
36 (Spain's FC Barcelona Ronaldinh/TORU YAMANAKA), 37 (Uruguay's
footballer Luis Suarez/MARTIN BERNETT), 37 (Uruguayan forward Luis
Suarez/ANTONIO SCORZA), 38 (Manchester City v Reading/Ian Walton),
38 (Bayern Munich's goalkeeper/BORIS HORVAT), 38 (Manchester United v
Chelsea/John Peters), 41 (Fluminense v Sao Paulo/Buda Mendes), 42 (UEFA
Champions League: Valencia v Inter Milan/Jamie McDonald), 44 (Manchester
United's Dutch goalkeeper/FRANCK FIFE), 46 (Napoli v AC Chievo Verona/
Giuseppe Bellini), 46 (Deportivo La Coruna v Barcelona/Angel Martinez),
49 (FIFA Confederations Cup 2009 – Brazil vs. Italy/Xu Suhui), 49 (Malaga CF
v FC Barcelona – Liga BBVA/David Ramos), 52 (Coach instructing teenage
male/Rana Faure), 53 (Javier Hernandez of Mexico celebrates/STAN HONDA),
54 (Italian footballer Mario Balotelli/ANDREW YATES), 54 (Arsenal's French
coach/ANDREAS SOLARO), 54 (Real Madrid's Portuguese coach Jose Mour/
JAVIER SORIANO), 56 (Suited man sitting on seat/Michael Blann), 57 (Football
coach in front of goal/John Giustina), 59 (Manchester United v Juventus/
Matthew Peters), 60 (Soccer referee/Image Source), 60 (Real Madrid's
Portuguese/PEDRO ARMESTRE), 62 (Barcelona v Real Madrid/David Ramos),
62 (Bayer 04 Leverkusen v FC Barcelona/Lars Baron), 63 (Rijkaard, Van Basten/
Bob Thomas), 66 (Manchester United v Fenerbahce/Tom Purslow), 66 (Brazil's
Rivaldo/CHRISTOPHE SIMON), 67 (The Italian referee Pierluigi Collina/
MLADEN ANTONOV), 68 (UEFA Champions League Final/Sandra Behne),
69 (Former Brazilian player Pele/FRANCK FIFE), 70 (Euro 2012 Qualifier –
Netherlands/VI-Images), 70 (Tottenham Hotspur's Welsh defender/GLYN
KIRK), 70 (Spain v Switzerland/Laurence Griffiths), 71 (United States v
Guadeloupe/Al Messerschmidt), 71 (Germany v Ukraine – International
Friendly/Joern Pollex), 73 (Football boots/Hugh Threlfall), 82 (Cristiano
Ronaldo/Angel Martinez); Offside sports Photography pp.6, 12 (all), 14 (warm
up, jump, mark), 18 (corner, goal kick, goal dive), 21, 22 (Jack Wilshire, Nani),
22, 23 (Beckham), 24, 30, 32, 33 (Segura, Cruijff), 35, 38 (d), 41 (Chilavert),
42 (Truman, Cech), 43 (top), 45, 46 (a,b,d), 49 (a,c,e), 52 (skills spot), 54 (c,e,f),
61, 62 (a,c,e), 63 (Sachi), 69 (a), 71 (c,d), 72 (a,b), 73 (a,b) ; Oxford University
Press pp.7 (Portrait of a boy/Score by Aflo), 10 (man in blue jacket/Image
Source), 10 (Man standing up smiling/Imageshop), 10 (Portrait of a woman
smiling/Radius Images), 10 (Portrait of a Business man/Image Source),
10 (Woman Broadcasting/Dave and Les Jacobs), 12 (man using mobile/i love
images); Press Association Images pp.14 (Manchester United/Ap/Press
Association images), 33 (Alfredo Di Stefano, Real Madrid and Spain), 71 (player
performing a back heel); Rex Features p.30 (Tottenham Hotspur Vs Aston Villa).

Commissioned Photography; Mark Mason Studios: p.12, p.73 (Armband/Mark
Mason Studios)

Cover images courtesy: Corbis, Red flag on soccer field; Getty Images,
Javier Hernandez of Manchester United (Laurence Griffiths), Lionel Messi
(Jose Jordon).

Illustrations by: Anne Cakebread pp.6, 8, 14, 18, 20, 22, 25, 27, 28, 38, 50, 55,
61; Peters and Zabransky pp.11, 16, 19, 26, 48, 58; Stefan Chabluk p.39

*The authors and publishers would like to thank the following for their help and support in
developing the book:* Manchester United FC, Liverpool FC, Stoke City FC, Bolton
Wanderers FC, Dale Hobson, Tony Wright and David Pepper at CMT Learning,
Eric Steele, Ben Amos, David De Gea, Javier Hernandez, Ji-Sun Park, Fabio Da
Silva, Rafael Da Silva, Federico Macheda, Paul Pogba, Davide Petrucci, Alberto
Massacci, Michele Fornasier, Charni Ekangamene, Gyliano Van Velzen, Adnan
Januzaj, Pierluigi Gollini, Michele Nastro, Hinrich Tode, Alexander Petrov, Sir
Alex Ferguson, Dave Bushell, Marek Szmid, Aidan Maloney, Jim Lawler, Lynne
Laffin, Bill & Judith Godfrey (Manchester Language School) Carmen Manzo
Warren, Michael Cox, Josep Segura, Rodolfo Borrell, Frank McParland, Mark
Morris, Clive Cook, Phil Roscoe, Ray Haughan, Jane Ashton, Amanda Eldridge,
Amy Smith, Greg Briggs, Lynda Watt, Mike Dickinson, Bill Ellaby, Tim Devine,
Trish Keppie, Lucas Leiva, Ariana Leiva, Martin Skrtel, Luis Suarez, Denis
Stracqualursi, Christine Redmond, Rob Sved, Jan Pizzey, Alvaro Arbeloa, Barry
Lewtas, Sebastian Coates, Felipe Forte, Jan Mucha, Barry O Connell, Andrea
Bernardi, Kristian Populin, Ryan McLaughlin, Steve Cooper, Stuart Webber,
Kristoffer Peterson, Peter Quinlivan, The Redmond and Nelson families, Austin
Ryan, Bjorn Baillie, Simon Baillie, Nicky Haworth, Fernando Torres, Rafael Leao,
Dave Grant, George Weber and Issy Michalski at Nike, Dale and Travis Phillips,
Garry Nelson, Dan Collins, Chris England, Patrick Cannon, Try Lingual Ltd.

Contents

About the book

English for Football has been developed specifically for people working in, or preparing to work in, the football industry who need to use English every day at work to communicate. The book will equip learners with the language skills and vocabulary necessary to understand typical situations in a football context.

English for Football consists of eight units. The book covers all the key positions on and off the pitch, from striker to manager. Units from the book work independently and can be selected according to the needs and interests of the course participants. *English for Football* can also be used for self-study.

Each unit begins with a **Kick-off**, which consists of a short exercise or quiz and serves as an introduction to the topic of the unit. Practical exercises, listening extracts, industry-specific texts, as well as photos and illustrations help you to acquire key vocabulary and expressions. Each unit closes with a **Profile** of a famous player followed by questions for reflection and discussion.

When you have completed the whole book you can **Test Yourself!** with the crossword on pages 70–71. In the appendix of *English for Football* you will also find a **Boardgame**, and the **Answer key** so that you can check your own answers if you are working alone. There are **Transcripts** of the **Listening extracts**. There is also an **A–Z wordlist** with all the key words that appear in *English for Football*. This includes a column of phonetics.

The **MultiROM** contains all the **Listening extracts** from the book. These can be played through the audio player on your computer, or through a conventional CD player. The **Interactive exercises** let you review your learning by doing exercises that cover the essential language from the book on your computer. This will be particularly valuable if you are using the book for self-study.

Foreword

by Sir Alex Ferguson

FOOTBALL today is a truly global phenomenon. Games are broadcast to vast audiences around the world, and replica team shirts are often worn in countries many thousands of kilometres from the clubs themselves. Players and staff increasingly migrate in pursuit of their careers; you only have to look at the composition of teams competing in the Champions League in Europe to see that.

Just as in business or science, in football too, people increasingly tend to use English to communicate. Significantly, this is also true of many football nations outside the English-speaking world where there are foreign players, coaches and so on.

In my own experience, I cannot stress how important it is for foreign players to be able to communicate with the coaching staff, medical team and team-mates in English both on and off the field.

Furthermore, it's fundamental for a player's integration that he can communicate confidently with fans, the media and with people in everyday situations. I am convinced this book will ease this adaptation process.

Moreover, I am sure it will also appeal to many speakers of other languages all over the world who simply wish to improve their knowledge of football-related English, or who just want to make learning English fun.

Sir Alex Ferguson CBE

UNIT 01

It's my club

Kick-off

1 Who are the players?

A B C D E F

2 Which positions do they play?

1 goalkeeper	3 full-back	5 winger
2 central defender	4 midfielder	6 striker

3 Look at the player positions below.

goalkeeper

right-back

central defender   central defender

left-back

right winger

midfielder

midfielder

striker

striker

left winger

4 Choose a famous player for each position.

Andrés Iniesta is a midfielder.

Reading

1 Complete the table about you.

	You	Carlo
Age		
Nationality		
Position		
Favourite team		
Favourite player		

2 Read and complete the table above about Carlo.

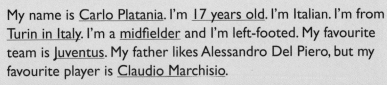

My name is <u>Carlo Platania</u>. I'm <u>17 years old</u>. I'm Italian. I'm from <u>Turin in Italy</u>. I'm a <u>midfielder</u> and I'm left-footed. My favourite team is <u>Juventus</u>. My father likes Alessandro Del Piero, but my favourite player is <u>Claudio Marchisio</u>.

3 Make questions for the answers <u>underlined</u> above.

What's your name?   *Carlo Platania*

Speaking

1 Practise asking and answering the questions.

1 What's your name?
2 How old are you?
3 Where are you from?
4 What position are you?
5 Are you left-footed or right-footed?
6 What's your favourite team?
7 Who's your favourite player?

Vocabulary

1 Complete the labels using the words below.

corner flag   penalty area   halfway line   bench
centre circle   sideline   six-yard box   by-line

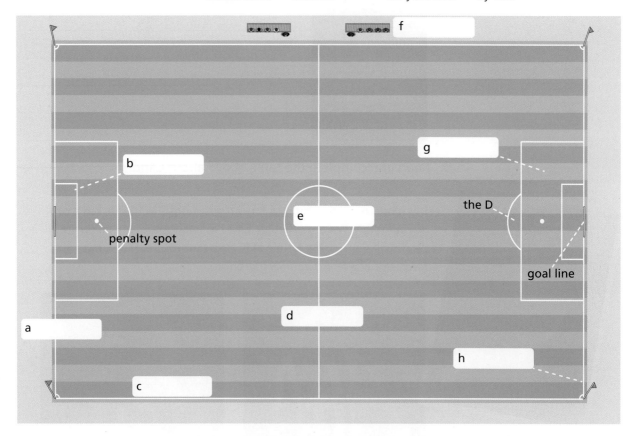

the D

penalty spot

goal line

2 ⊙ 02 Read and listen to the numbers.

0 1 2 3 4 5 6 7 8 9 10 11 12 13 14 15 16 17 18 19 20
30 40 50 60 70 80 90 100

3 Match the questions to the answers.

1 How many players are there in a team?	a 3
2 How long is a game of football?	b 10
3 Which number is Maradona famous for?	c every 4 years
4 How many goals are there in a hat-trick?	d 11
5 How often is the World Cup?	e 90 minutes
6 What number is the goalkeeper in English teams?	f 1

Did you know?

When we say football scores, we use *nil* instead of *zero* i.e. 2-0:
   The score is two-nil.
When the score is 1-1, we say *It's one-all.*

4 ⊙ 03 Listen and complete the results.

1 Real Madrid ____ – 0 Bayern Munich
2 Ajax 3 – ____ Shakhtar Donetsk
3 Chelsea ____ – 1 AC Milan
4 Porto 0 – ____ Lyon

5 Now practise saying the scores.

Reading

1 Read. Are the sentences True (**T**) or False (**F**)?

1	The German first division is the Bundesliga.	T
2	Edison Arantes do Nascimento is the real name of Ronaldinho.	F
3	Manchester United are *The Red Devils*.	
4	Substitutes are on the bench at the start of a game.	
5	Real Madrid v Barcelona is called *El Grande* in Spain.	
6	The Maracana is the biggest stadium in Europe.	
7	Diego Maradona's middle name is Gabriel.	
8	The San Siro is the home stadium of AC Milan and Internazionale.	
9	The original World Cup trophy is the Jules Rimet.	
10	The French national team are *The Lions*.	

Language

PRESENT SIMPLE: *to be*

Affirmative		Negative		Question	
I'm a		**I'm not**		**Am I**	
You're a	winger.	**You aren't**		**Are you**	
He's a		**He isn't**	tall.	**Is he**	in the team?
They're	wingers.	**They aren't**		**Are they**	

- We use the plural when we talk about teams in English.

  Chelsea **are** my favourite team. **NOT** ~~Chelsea is my favourite team.~~
  Why **are** Barcelona so good?

Practice

1 Read and write *Yes, it is / Yes, he is.* or *No, it isn't. / No, he isn't.*

1 Is Cristiano Ronaldo Spanish? ___No, he isn't.___

2 Is the Bernabeu Stadium in Italy? _____

3 Is Wesley Sneijder a defender? _____

4 Is the Champions League for European teams? _____

5 Is Yaya Toure from Ivory Coast? _____

2 Complete the sentences with *is, isn't, are.*

1 Sergio Aguero _____is_____ a striker.

2 How old _____ you?

3 Napoli _____ an Italian team.

4 Wembley Stadium _____ in Manchester.

5 The semi-finals _____ next weekend.

6 Who _____ the Under-21 world champions?

Listening

1 Match the words to the pictures.

1 journalist   3 manager   5 linesman
2 referee   4 supporter   6 physio

2 ⊙ 04 Listen and match.

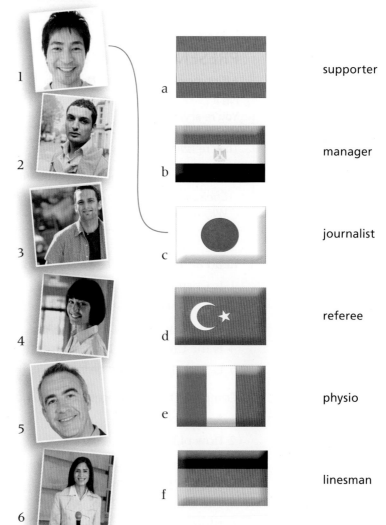

1
2
3
4
5
6

a   supporter
b   manager
c   journalist
d   referee
e   physio
f   linesman

3 Make sentences.

Howard Webb is a referee. He's from England.

Vocabulary

1 Write the parts of the body using the vocabulary below.

head	shin
arm	chest
mouth	fingers
leg	nose
shoulder	stomach
hand	ear
foot	ankle
eye	toes
knee	elbow
hair	neck

2 Complete the sentences with the body parts below.

chest   feet   foot   hand   elbow   arms

1 I can control the ball with my _____chest_____.

2 Is that a _____-ball?

3 Many goalkeepers have long _____.

4 Nani is famous for his quick _____.

5 The defender fouls him with his _____.

6 Arjen Robben shoots with his left _____.

3 Write the correct verb under each picture.

kick   pass   shoot   head   tackle   foul

_____

_____

_____

_____

_____

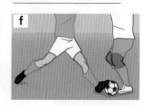

_____

Everyday English Greetings and introductions

1 ⊙ 05 Listen to Bolaji in three situations. Who is Bolaji talking to each time?

2 Listen again and complete the dialogues.

Dialogue 1

A: Bolaji, come and meet Mr Turner.

B: Hi, I'm the Academy Manager – Harry Turner. ¹_____ to England, Bolaji!

C: Thank you! ²_____ Mr Turner!

B: Call me Harry!

C: OK, Harry!

Dialogue 2

A: Hi, are you the new striker?

B: No, I'm a defender.

A: I'm Conor, the kitman.

B: Bolaji!

A: Where ³_____, Bolaji?

B: ⁴_____ Nigeria. Where are you from?

A: Ireland. Here you are son: shirt, shorts, two pairs of socks…

Dialogue 3

A: ⁵_____, Bolaji!

B: Thanks, Gaffer!

A: Who's that, son?

B: Oh, ⁶_____ my father, Boss.

A: Hi, pleased to meet you!

C: ⁷_____ .

3 Practise reading the dialogues.

4 Match the words below with the items of kit.

1 armband	3 boots	5 hat	7 shin pads	9 socks
2 bib	4 gloves	6 shirt	8 shorts	10 training bottoms

5 Answer the questions.

1 What colour is the shirt? __It's red and white.__

2 What colour are the socks? __They're_____

3 What colour are the gloves? _____

4 What colour is the hat? _____

5 What colour are the shorts? _____

6 What colour are the boots? _____

Profile

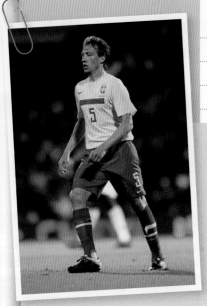

Lucas Leiva

English student and professional footballer

Date of birth:	9 January, 1987
Place of birth:	Dourados, Brazil
Height:	1.79 metres
Position:	Midfielder

Are you happy with your English?

Yes, I'm very happy. It's difficult moving from Brazil to England. The weather is different, the food is different, the style of football is different and, of course, the language is different – in Brazil we speak Portuguese. I can't change the weather, but I can improve my English!

Is it a dream to wear the yellow shirt of Brazil?

Absolutely. I think that most people in the world are fans of Brazil! Our shirt is the most famous shirt in football. Everybody knows about the great Brazilian players of the past like Pelé, Jairzinho, Zico, Romario, Cafu, Roberto Carlos, Ronaldo and Ronaldinho. It's a very long list.

Is it difficult to learn football vocabulary in English?

A little, but I need to understand my team-mates so I want to continue to learn quickly.

What is your advice to footballers and football fans who want to learn English?

You need to concentrate in class! Ask your teacher questions if you don't understand, and read as much English as possible.

What's your favourite English word or expression?

I like the word *mate*. It means friend. Everybody says this in Liverpool.

Speaking Discussion

1 Do you agree with these sentences?

1 All good players can play well with both feet.

2 Strikers are more important than defenders.

3 South American strikers are the best in the world.

4 A referee has a harder job than a footballer.

Defender

Kick-off

1 Who is your favourite defender? Which position does he play?

2 Who are the players below? Are they full-backs or central defenders?

A

B

C

D

E

F

3 Match the verbs with the pictures above.

1 block	3 warm up	5 clear
2 mark	4 shake hands	6 jump

Did you know? ⚽

We also call a central defender a *centre half* or a *centre back*.

4 Look at the examples below. Talk about your favourite full-back and your favourite central defender.

Ashley Cole is good at tackling and passing.

Vincent Kompany is good at jumping and clearing.

SKILLS SPOT

Slide tackle

Defenders have to be good at tackling. This is a slide tackle. Be careful not to foul the other player! It is sometimes called a sliding tackle.

Reading

1 What do you do before and after a game?

2 Read about Marek.

Before, during, and after

This is **Marek Jaworski**. He's a defender from Poland. He's a centre half. He's tall and he's good in the air. We asked him three questions …

What do you do before a game?

I like to listen to music. It's important to relax. Then, I warm up for 30 minutes.

Do you talk during a game?

During a game, I talk to my team-mates a lot. I'm the captain of our team. When the ball is in our penalty area, I shout 'Clear it!' Before a corner or a free-kick, I shout 'Mark up!'

What is the first thing you do after a game?

After a game, I always shake hands with the referee and the players of the other team.

3 Answer the questions.

1 What position is Marek?
2 What two things does he do before a game?
3 What does he say to his team-mates during a game?
4 What does he always do after a game?

Language

PRESENT SIMPLE

Affirmative			Negative		
I/You	**train**		I/You	**don't train**	
He/She	**train<u>s</u>**	every day.	He/She	**doesn't train**	every day.
We/They	**train**		We/They	**don't train**	

- We use the Present Simple when we speak about what normally happens.
  *He usually **plays** on Saturdays.   He **doesn't tackle** well.*

- We also use the Present Simple to speak about facts.
  *Bayern Munich **wear** red shirts.   Chelsea **don't play** in the Primera Liga.*

Practice

1 Complete the sentences with the correct form of the verb in brackets.

1 I _____get up_____ (get up) at seven o'clock.
2 Goalkeepers _____ (wear) gloves.
3 They _____ (speak) Portuguese in Brazil.
4 We _____ (not have) a lot of supporters.
5 Our manager _____ (like) to win 1-0!
6 You're a good player because you _____ (work) very hard.
7 This referee _____ (not give) penalties.
8 I _____ (not like) the gym.

Listening

1 Match the phrases with the pictures.

1 go to the gym
2 practise set-pieces
3 practise heading

4 play a five-a-side game
5 name the team
6 have a day off

 A

 B

 C

 D

 E

 F

2 What is your favourite day of the week? Why? What is your favourite time of day: morning, afternoon or evening?

3 ⊙ 06 Listen to Nicky, a defender, speaking about his routine. Then complete the table.

Day	Activities
	He runs and practises set-pieces. He plays a short game on the indoor pitch.
	The manager talks about tactics before the match. He plays the match.
	He trains in the morning. He watches a video of his opponents.
	He plays pool or video games. He watches football on TV.
	He practises heading the ball. He goes in the swimming pool.
Monday	He goes to the gym in the morning. He plays a practice match.
	He plays a five-a-side game. The manager names the team for Saturday's game.

4 Ask questions about Nicky's week.   *What does Nicky do on Mondays?*

Reading

1 How many points does your team get when you win a game? And when you draw a game?

2 Read about Yalany.

I'm Yalany and I'm a defender. I play at left-back. Players in the other team never get past me! I come from Guinea-Bissau, but I live in Scotland. It always rains here, but I like it. I play for a good team. I like our number 10. He usually plays behind the striker. He's often our best player. We sometimes win home games 3-0 or 3-1. When we get three points everybody's happy. But we sometimes lose, and our coach is very unhappy! When we draw away, he's happy with the point.

3 Read. Are the sentences True (**T**) or False (**F**)?

1 Yalany thinks it rains all the time in Scotland. ___

2 The number 10 usually plays in front of the striker. ___

3 The number 10 is always the best player. ___

4 Yalany's team win all their games. ___

Language

ADVERBS OF FREQUENCY

These are words that we use to describe how often we do something.

○○○○	●○○○	●●○○	●●●○	●●●●
never	sometimes	often	usually	always

How often do you use your left foot?
I'm left-footed, so I **usually** use my left foot.

How often do you play tennis?
I don't like tennis. I **never** play tennis.

Practice

1 Complete the sentences about Yalany.

1 The other players ___never___ get past Yalany.

2 It _____ rains in Scotland.

3 The number 10 _____ plays behind the striker.

4 The number 10 is _____ their best player.

5 Yalany's team _____ win their home games 3-0.

Did you know?

When your team play on your pitch, it's a *home game*. When you play on another team's pitch, it's an *away game*.

Vocabulary

1 Match the words with the pictures.

1 penalty 2 corner 3 throw-in 4 free-kick 5 goal kick

2 These are called set-pieces. Which players take the set-pieces for your favourite team?

1 _____ takes the free-kicks for _____.

2 _____ takes the penalties for _____.

3 _____ takes the corners for _____.

4 _____ takes the throw-ins for _____.

5 _____ takes the goal kicks for _____.

3 How often do you take set-pieces?

1 I _____ take free-kicks.   4 I _____ take throw-ins.

2 I _____ take penalties.   5 I _____ take goal kicks.

3 I _____ take corners.

Listening

1 Look at the picture showing the positions of the goal.

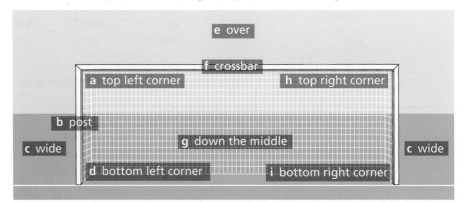

2 ⊙ 07 Now listen and write the letters.

1 ___ 2 ___ 3 ___ 4 ___ 5 ___ 6 ___ 7 ___ 8 ___ 9 ___

3 When you take a penalty, where do you kick the ball?

I always try for the top right corner.

Listening

1 Make sentences about Lilian Thuram.

1 Lilian Thuram	a Parma, Juventus and France.
2 He played for	b 1998 World Cup semi-final against Croatia.
3 Thuram only scored two goals	c for his country.
4 His two goals came in the	d is a defender.

2 ⊙ 08 Listen to the commentaries of Thuram's goals. Complete the sentences.

Goal 1

1 Thuram _____ the Croatian defender.
2 Thuram _____ the ball.
3 Djorkaeff _____ it back to Thuram.
4 Thuram _____ for France.

Goal 2

1 Zidane _____ the ball to Lilian Thuram.
2 Thuram _____ forward and passes to a French player.
3 Thuram _____ from outside the area.

Reading

1 Look at each sequence. Match the phrases to the correct picture.

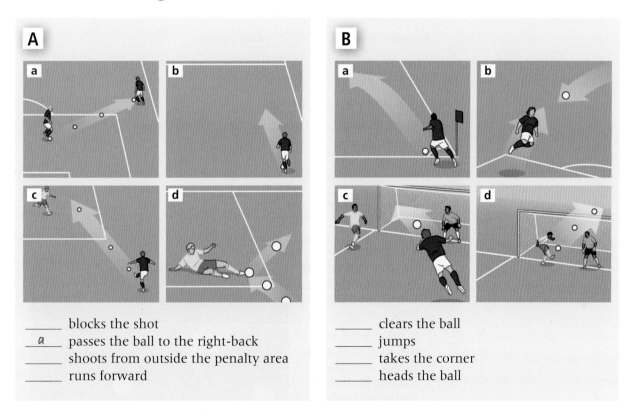

A

_____ blocks the shot
__a__ passes the ball to the right-back
_____ shoots from outside the penalty area
_____ runs forward

B

_____ clears the ball
_____ jumps
_____ takes the corner
_____ heads the ball

2 Give names to the players in the sequence. Practise a commentary.

Fàbregas passes the ball to the right-back.

Everyday English Likes and dislikes

1 ◎ 09 Listen to Jérémie in three situations. What are the people talking about each time?

2 Listen again and complete the dialogues. What expressions are used to express likes and dislikes?

Dialogue 1

A: ¹_____ the new kit, Jérémie?

B: ²_____

A: It's great! It's like the Milan kit.

B: Exactly. I prefer Inter. ³_____ those colours!

Dialogue 2

A: Jérémie, do you want some more potatoes?

B: Yes, please. ⁴_____ vegetables.

A: ⁵_____ them. Here, have mine!

Dialogue 3

A: Jérémie, it's defenders against strikers in training today.

B: Fantastic. I ⁶_____!

A: I know, but the boss ⁷_____ when you go forward in a real game.

B: Well, he ⁸_____ when I score!

3 Practise reading the dialogues.

4 Make sentences about you.

*I love …   I like …   I don't mind …   I don't like …   I hate …
I can't stand …*

SKILLS SPOT

Nutmeg

If a player kicks the ball through the legs of an opposition player, he *nutmegs* him.

In other languages this is often called a tunnel. In England, *nutmeg* is often shortened to *megs*.

Profile

Fabio and Rafael Da Silva

English students and professional footballers

Date of birth:	9 July, 1990
Place of birth:	Petropolis, Rio de Janeiro, Brazil
Height:	1.72 metres
Position:	Full-back

Was it hard to learn the language when you came to England?

RAFAEL: Yes, it was difficult, and we still make mistakes. But we can communicate quite well in English now. We can tell jokes too!

FABIO: I'm sometimes nervous when I speak English – sometimes I am more nervous than when I play a big Champions League match!

You're twin brothers. Does being together make life easier?

FABIO: Definitely! We help each other a lot. We're both full-backs so we help each other in training and before games ...

RAFAEL: But not in our English lessons! We're very competitive!

Physically, you are very similar. Are you similar in character?

RAFAEL: We're different but we're very close. In fact, when one of us is on the bench for a game, we get really nervous for the other one who's playing. But when we play, it's OK!

What's it like playing football in Europe?

RAFAEL: It's a different style of football, especially for a Brazilian full-back. At home, we usually attacked. My brother scored a lot of goals!

FABIO: Players here are very big and very strong, too. And you need to concentrate for 90 minutes! But training in cold weather is much better than in 40 degrees in Brazil!

And what about life in England?

RAFAEL: It's good. Our wives and family are here too. We can eat our favourite food here and watch our favourite Brazilian TV channel.

FABIO: We're Brazilian and we love our country, so we sometimes miss home. But our house is usually full of people. It sometimes feels like our home town!

Speaking   Discussion

1 Do you agree with these sentences?

1 A good team has defenders who can score goals.

2 Defenders are stronger than players in other positions.

3 European defenders are the best in the world.

4 Defenders are the best captains, because they put the team's interests ahead of their own.

Midfielder

Kick-off

1 What formation does your favourite team use?

2 Name each of the formations below.

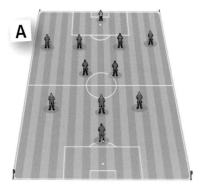

A

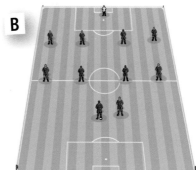

B

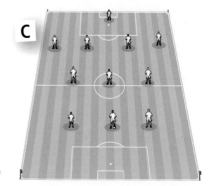

C

3 Read and match the players to the formations.

Michael

My team plays with a classic English formation. In midfield we have two wingers and two central midfielders. We have four defenders and two strikers.

Robbie

We play attacking football, and we like to pass and move. My team plays with four defenders, three midfield players and three forwards.

Amir

We have two defensive midfielders, three attacking midfielders and one striker. One of our attacking midfielders plays in the number 10 position. He is the creative player in the team.

4 What kind of midfielders do you think these players are?

defensive midfielder   central midfielder   winger   attacking midfielder

Jack Wilshere

Nani

Michael Essien

Andrés Iniesta

Reading

1 Which midfielders help the defence for your favourite team?

2 Read the article. Do you agree with the journalist? Who is your favourite midfielder?

Midfield maestros

Name: Ryan Giggs
Position: winger

This is my favourite player of all time. He has more winners' medals in English football than any other player. Ryan Giggs is a classic winger. He runs, he dribbles, he crosses the ball, but he also defends. He has an amazing record of scoring in every season of the Premier League.

Name: Zinedine Zidane
Position: number 10

This is my favourite position on the pitch, and the classic number 10 is Zinedine Zidane. What a genius! He moved between the midfielders and the strikers to create chances. He also scored lots of important goals, like his goals in the 1998 World Cup Final.

Name: Claude Makélélé
Position: defensive midfielder

One of the best defensive midfielders is Claude Makélélé. In fact, a lot of people call this position the 'Makélélé role'! Real Madrid legend Fernando Hierro says that Makélélé was the best player in the Real Madrid team that included Zinedine Zidane, Ronaldo, Luís Figo and Raúl!

Name: Xavi Hernández
Position: central midfielder

For me, Xavi Hernández is the best passer of the ball in the history of football! He completed 148 passes in the 2011 Champions League Final. He is always looking around him. During a game, he moves his head from side to side all the time!

3 Read again and name the player.

1 He's the best passer of the ball.

2 He's the journalist's favourite player.

3 He plays in the journalist's favourite position.

4 People sometimes call the defensive midfielder role after him.

5 He is always looking around him.

6 He played between the midfielders and the strikers.

Reading

1 Which famous players wear the number 10 shirt?

2 Read this article about the number 10 position.

The Number 10

by Michael Cox,
www.zonalmarking.net

Pelé and Diego Maradona made the number 10 shirt famous. But it is sometimes difficult to understand the number 10 position. When we talk about the number 10 we are not always talking about the number on the shirt. We are talking about the footballer's job in the team.

Wayne Rooney, for example, wears the number 10 shirt, but he is not a number 10. He's a second striker.

We often see a number 10 in teams with a 4-2-3-1 formation. But the number 10 is not a player who runs forward from the centre of midfield, like Frank Lampard or Andrés Iniesta.

A number 10 plays in front of the midfielders and behind the strikers. He is the most important creative player in the team. He doesn't need to run past players, and he doesn't always score a lot of goals. He finds space on the pitch and helps to create chances. Luka Modric and David Silva often play in the number 10 position.

Many fantastic number 10s come from Argentina. One of my favourites is Juan Riquelme. In fact, he is my perfect number 10!

3 Answer the questions.

1 Why is it difficult to understand the number 10 position?

2 Does Michael think Wayne Rooney is a number 10?

3 Does a number 10 run forward from the centre of midfield?

4 Where does a number 10 play on the pitch?

5 Does a number 10 always run past players?

6 How does a number 10 help the team?

7 Who is Michael's perfect number 10?

4 Complete the sentences using the prepositions below.

into   behind   on   past   in front of   in   from

1 Andrés Iniesta and Frank Lampard like to run forward _from_ the centre of midfield.

2 Gareth Bale is very fast. It's easy for him to get _____ the defender.

3 Wesley Sneijder is a number 10. He plays _____ the striker.

4 Cesc Fàbregas plays _____ midfield, but he scores a lot of goals.

5 Lucas Leiva is a defensive midfielder. He plays _____ the defence.

6 Park Ji-Sung runs _____ the penalty area and scores a great goal!

7 I enjoy playing _____ the wing, like my hero Ryan Giggs!

Listening

1 ⊙ 10 Listen to Paco and complete the factfile.

FACTFILE

Name:	Paco
Nationality:	_____
Age:	_____
Position:	central midfielder
Favourite player:	_____
Likes:	video games and _____
Dislikes:	_____

Did you know?

When a coach wants you to move into a more defensive position, he says *Come deep! Drop deep!* or *Track back!*

2 Listen again. Are the sentences about Paco's life in England True (**T**) or False (**F**)?

1 Paco is playing at an academy. ___

2 He is playing as a central midfielder. ___

3 He is training more with the ball. ___

4 He is defending for the team more. ___

5 He isn't enjoying himself. ___

SKILLS SPOT

La roulette

This is a famous skill used by Zinedine Zidane, Ronaldinho and Diego Maradona. First you run to the ball and move the ball towards you with one foot. Then turn while you use the other foot to move away from the defender.

Reading

1 Match the electronic boards with the information.

1 United are losing.

2 Number 4 is coming off.

3 They are playing four minutes of additional time.

4 United are winning.

5 Number 4 is coming on.

6 United are drawing.

Language

PRESENT CONTINUOUS: BE + *ING*

Affirmative	Negative	Question
I'm playing.	I'm not playing.	Am I playing?
He's playing.	He isn't playing.	Is he playing?

- We use the Present Continuous to talk about things that are happening now.
  What are you doing?   I'm studying English at the moment.

- We also use the Present Continuous for things that are happening around now, but not necessarily at this moment.
  What are you doing in training?   We are working on set-pieces.

- We also use the Present Continuous for future plans.
  Where are we playing next week?   We are playing at home.

Practice

1 Complete the sentences using the Present Continuous.

1 Luka Modrić _____is calling_____ (call) for the ball.

2 We _____ (play) away next weekend.

3 Cristiano Ronaldo _____ (run) down the wing.

4 Who _____ (you train) with?

5 They _____ (do) very well this season.

6 Mesut Özil _____ (look) for a team-mate.

2 Write sentences that are true for you at the moment.

1 I / wearing my kit
  I'm not wearing my kit. I'm wearing jeans and a T-shirt.

2 I / sitting on the bench _____

3 It / raining _____

4 We / working in the gym _____

5 I / sending a text message _____

6 My friends / playing video games _____

Vocabulary

1 Look at the diagrams. Match each one to a description below.

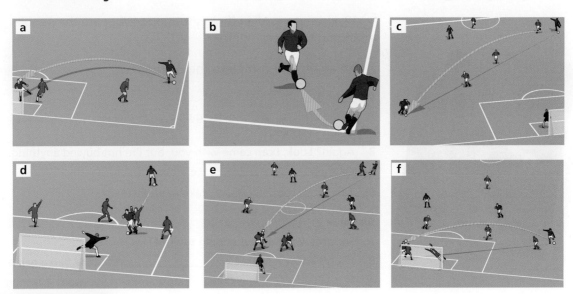

1 Mateusz is crossing the ball to the back post.

2 Jo is playing a short pass.

3 Nico is playing a long ball.

4 Kaito is crossing the ball to the front post.

5 Juan is playing a through ball.

6 Ali is playing a diagonal pass.

Listening

1 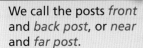 11 Listen to a coach giving instructions to Dragoslav and Ken-zhi before a game. Which player is a substitute today?

2 ⊙ Listen again. Circle the correct player each time.

1 *Dragoslav* / *Ken-zhi* is taking the throw-ins.

2 *Dragoslav* / *Ken-zhi* is playing in central midfield.

3 *Dragoslav* / *Ken-zhi* is good at tackling.

4 *Dragoslav* / *Ken-zhi* is right-footed.

5 *Dragoslav* / *Ken-zhi* is playing on the left wing.

6 *Dragoslav* / *Ken-zhi* is coming on for the second half.

3 Match the two parts of each instruction below.

1 It's not a foul!

2 Pass the ball!

3 Don't pass the ball!

4 Take the throw!

5 Kick the ball out of play!

6 Warm up!

a The striker's free!

b The striker's offside!

c It's our ball!

d You're coming on!

e Play on!

f The striker's injured!

Everyday English Making arrangements

1 ⊙ 12 Listen to Jordi in three situations. What are the people arranging to do each time?

2 Listen again and complete the dialogues.

Dialogue 1

A: Come on Jordi, we're getting paid on Friday. ¹_____ going shopping?

B: Again? Look, I can come with you, but I'm not buying anything.

A: OK. ²_____ take a taxi!

B: Taxi? ³_____ take a bus instead?

Dialogue 2

A: So Jordi, what are you doing tonight?

B: I don't know really. ⁴_____ watch the Barça game?

A: ⁵_____. Come round to mine if you want. My mum won't mind.

B: Yeah, ⁶_____!

Dialogue 3

A: Jordi, it's your first interview this afternoon, OK?

B: ⁷_____, but is it in English?

A: Yes, of course it's in English! ⁸_____ prepare for it together!

B: Thanks, I need your help.

A: ⁹_____ in the canteen at two o'clock!

SKILLS SPOT

Cut inside

Wingers often *cut inside* when they want to shoot. When a right winger is running down the wing with the ball, sometimes he quickly moves to the left, or *cuts inside*. This surprises the defender and the winger can shoot. Arjen Robben does this a lot.

Profile

Paul Pogba

English student and professional footballer

Date of birth:	15 March, 1993
Place of birth:	Lagny-sur-Marne, France
Height:	1.91 metres
Position:	Midfielder

Did you speak English when you arrived in Manchester?

No, very little actually, and it was difficult at first. But now I'm always talking at the training ground and making jokes! I'm learning all the time – even slang words. Also, I love the English word game, Scrabble. This helps me to learn new words. I have some English language certificates now. I keep them on my wall next to my first French national team shirt!

Which midfielders did you like when you were young?

Well, I liked Ronaldinho and Zidane because I played number 10. Then I changed position and started to understand how good Vieira was. I'm watching a lot of his videos at the moment.

Of course, people often compare you to Patrick Vieira. What was it like to play against him?

Yes, I played against him once at Paul Scholes's testimonial at Old Trafford. To be honest, I couldn't get near Patrick! His turns, his touch, his strength are all amazing. In French we say someone is 'too hot' when they are too good to play against!

What's the best advice you've ever had in football?

Well, I get a lot of advice from my two elder brothers – they're twins and they're both footballers like me. But I also love something that Xavi often says in interviews. He says he is always thinking about space, and always looking for it in a game. He also says that he feels 'lost' without the ball, and sometimes I feel the same!

Speaking Discussion

1 Do you agree with these sentences?

1 Midfielders run more than players in other positions.

2 The best teams are the teams with the best midfield.

3 Wingers are more skilful than central midfielders.

4 The most important thing for a midfielder is to keep possession.

 **Striker**

Kick-off

1 Which strikers are scoring lots of goals at the moment?

2 Look at the players below. Match the words with the pictures.

1 volley
2 overhead kick
3 long-range shot

4 back-heel
5 diving header
6 close-range shot

3 Which of the goals are easier to score and which are more difficult?

SKILLS SPOT

Finding the bottom corner

The best strikers have the ability to *find the bottom corner*. Great players can place the ball just inside the post and out of the keeper's reach.

Reading

1 Read about Roger Milla. Then complete the table.

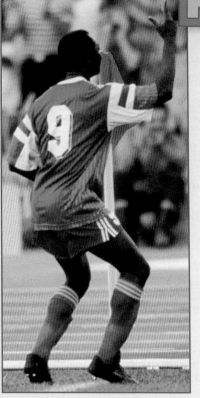

ROGER MILLA AT THE WORLD CUP

1982

In Spain in 1982, Cameroon played in the World Cup for the first time. They played against Peru in their first game. Roger Milla scored, but his goal was disallowed. The game ended 0-0. Cameroon also drew their next two games. They didn't qualify for the second round, but everybody liked the bright colours of the Cameroon kit and their supporters were fantastic! Roger didn't get his name on the scoresheet, but people noticed him. Italy were the competition winners.

1990

In 1990, the World Cup was in Italy. Cameroon qualified for the second time in their history. This time they reached the quarter-finals. Germany won the tournament, but Roger scored four goals and became famous for his goal celebrations. Every time he scored, he ran to the corner flag and started dancing. Today, lots of players do this kind of thing, but Roger was the first!

1994

Roger made his last World Cup appearance four years later in the USA. Brazil won the tournament. Cameroon didn't play well and they went out in the first round. In one game, Cameroon lost 6-1 to Russia. Oleg Salenko scored five goals in one match – a World Cup record. For Cameroon, Roger Milla broke a record too. He scored his only goal of the tournament and became the oldest goalscorer in the history of the World Cup. He was 42 years old!

Roger scored five goals at the World Cup between 1982 and 1994, and was later nominated as African Player of the Century. In 2004, Pelé included Roger on his FIFA 100 list of top players.

Year of World Cup	1982	1990	1994
Host nation	Spain		
World Cup winners		Germany	
Number of goals scored by Roger Milla			
Round when Cameroon were eliminated			1st round

2 Complete the text using the words below.

qualify   scoresheet   tournament
appearance   disallowed   celebrations

Cameroon also played at the 1998 World Cup. They needed to win their final group game against Chile. François Omam-Biyick scored a goal to make it 2-1, but the goal was [1]_____. Cameroon didn't [2]_____ for the second round. A 17-year-old called Samuel Eto'o made his first [3]_____ at this World Cup but he didn't get his name on the [4]_____. There were incredible [5]_____ when the host nation, France, won the [6]_____.

Language

PAST SIMPLE

Affirmative	Negative	Question
Roger **played** in three World Cups.	Roger **didn't play** in a World Cup Final.	**Did** Roger **play** in the 1994 World Cup?

- We use the Past Simple to talk about things that happened in the past.

  In 1982, Cameroon **qualified** *for the World Cup for the first time.*
  Most regular verbs end in *-ed* in the past simple.

  *Everybody **liked** the bright colours of the Cameroon kit.*

- There are many verbs that have irregular forms in the Past Simple.
  *Russia **beat** Cameroon 6-1.   They **drew** their next two games.*

Practice

1 Look at the article on page 31. <u>Underline</u> the Past Simple verbs.

2 Write the Past Simple form of the verbs below.

1 turn ___turned___   4 run _____   7 receive _____

2 score _____   5 be _____   8 shoot _____

3 help _____   6 have _____

3 Use the verbs above to complete the text about Diego Maradona.

People remember the 1986 World Cup for Diego Maradona. He [1]____had____ a fantastic tournament as Argentina captain, and he [2]_____ them win the competition for the second time. Maradona [3]_____ two of the most famous goals in football history, both against England in the quarter-finals. Many people say the second of these two goals [4]_____ the most beautiful goal of all time. Maradona [5]_____ the ball in his own half, then [6]_____, and [7]_____ more than 60 metres, past five English defenders and then [8]_____ into the bottom corner. What a goal!

4 Look at the final Brazilian league table for 2011. Complete the sentences using the verbs below. Use the Past Simple.

draw
score
play
win
concede
lose

		P	W	D	L	F	A	Pts
1	Corinthians	38	21	8	9	53	36	71
2	Vasco da Gama	38	19	12	7	57	40	69
3	Fluminense	38	20	3	15	60	51	63
4	Flamengo	38	15	16	7	59	47	61
5	Internacional	38	16	12	10	57	43	60
6	São Paulo	38	16	11	11	57	46	59

1 All of the teams _____ 38 games.

2 Fluminense _____ 15 games.

3 Flamengo _____ 59 goals.

4 Internacional _____ 12 games.

5 Vasco da Gama _____ 19 games.

6 Corinthians _____ 36 goals.

Listening

Josep Segura knows a lot about football. He has been coach at Barcelona's Academy, manager of Olympiakos, and Technical Director at Liverpool FC Academy. His favourite attacking players are Alfredo Di Stefano, Pelé, Johan Cruijff and Diego Maradona.

1 Read the statistics. Write sentences using the Past Simple.

Alfredo Di Stefano
Date of birth: 14 July, 1926
World Cup appearances: 0

1 _Di Stefano was born on 14 July, 1926._
2 _____

Pelé
World Cup winner: 3 times
Number of clubs: 2 (Santos and New York Cosmos)

1 _____
2 _____

Diego Maradona
Goals for Argentina: 34
Shirt number: 10

1 _____
2 _____

Johan Cruijff
Ajax debut: 15 November, 1964
Manager: Ajax, Barcelona, Netherlands, Catalonia

1 _____
2 _____

2 ⊙ 13 Listen to Josep talking about these players. Name one thing that Josep likes about each player.

3 Match the terms (1–5) with the definitions (a–e). Look at the transcript of the interview on page 90 to help you.

1 lose your man
2 dribble
3 composure
4 pace
5 good timing

a the ability to stay calm when you have a chance to score
b the ability to run fast
c to run with the ball past players
d the ability to run, jump, shoot, etc. at the right moment
e to free yourself from your marker

Did you know?

When the three goals in a hat-trick consist of one header, one goal scored with the right foot, and one goal scored with the left foot, this is called a *perfect hat-trick*.

Pronunciation

1 ⊙ 14 Listen and repeat the sentences from Josep's interview.

1 He *scored* all types of goals.

2 He also *created* lots of goals.

3 I *watched* him play every week.

2 ⊙ 15 The Past Simple ending *-ed* can be pronounced three different ways. Listen.

/t/	/d/	/ɪd/
watched	scored	created

3 Read the script of the interview on page 90. Find the regular verbs and write them in the correct column above.

4 Add two more verbs to each column.

Listening

1 ⊙ 16 Listen to the interview with a young striker called Andrew.

2 Read these sentences and listen again. Are they True (**T**) or False (**F**)?

1 People said Andrew was too short to be a striker. ___

2 Andrew is worried about his height. ___

3 He is taller than Sergio Aguero and Javier Hernández. ___

4 He says that Neymar and Luis Suárez have good pace and movement. ___

5 His favourite player when he was young was Raúl. ___

6 He was a goalkeeper before he became a striker. ___

Language

QUESTIONS USING THE PAST SIMPLE

- In the Present Simple, when we ask a question with a *Yes / No* answer, we use an auxiliary verb, *do*. In the Past Simple, we use the past form, *did*.

  ***Did** you think that your size was a problem?*

- If the main verb is *to be*, then we use a form of that verb.

  ***Were** you a goalkeeper once?*

- In all tenses, information questions start with a **question word** (*What / Which / When / Who / Where / Why / How*). These are questions in the Past Simple:

  ***Which** strikers **did** you like when you were younger?*
  ***Why did** you stop playing in goal?*

Practice **1** Complete the questions with the words below.

> What   Who   Who   Where   Why   How

1 ___How___ did they win the league? They're rubbish!
2 _____ did they beat last weekend?
3 _____ was it a late kick-off?
4 _____ was the score?
5 _____ was the final? Rome?
6 _____ scored the first goal?

Pronunciation **1** ◉ 17 Listen and repeat the questions. Notice the intonation.

When did you arrive here?   Which team did he play for?

2 ◉ 18 Listen and repeat the questions. Then underline the stressed words, or parts of words.

1 Did you <u>al</u>ways want to be a <u>foot</u>baller?
2 Did you think that your size was a problem?
3 Which strikers did you like when you were younger?
4 Were you a goalkeeper once?
5 Why did you stop playing in goal?

Listening **1** ◉ 19 Listen and complete the information about Lionel Messi.

FACTFILE: Lionel Messi

Full name: ¹_____
Nicknames: Leo, La Pulga (the flea), El Mudo (the mute)
Date of birth: ²_____
Place of birth: Rosario, Argentina
Height: ³_____   Position: ⁴_____
First club: Newell's Old Boys, Rosario
Record number of goals in a season: ⁵_____

2 Write questions for the answers about Cristiano Ronaldo.

1 ___What's his full name___? Cristiano Ronaldo dos Santos Aveiro.
2 _____? CR7.
3 _____? 5 February, 1985.
4 _____? Funchal, Madeira, Portugal.
5 _____? 1.86 metres.
6 _____? Winger/striker.
7 _____? Andorinha. Then he went to Sporting.
8 _____? 60 goals in all competitions (2011–2012).

Everyday English Apologizing and giving reasons

In English, if you make a mistake or get something wrong, it's polite to apologize and give a reason.

1 ⊙ 20 Listen to three dialogues. For each one, say why the person apologizes, and what reason they give.

2 Listen again and complete the dialogues.

Dialogue 1

A: Juan-Pablo! Glad you could make it this morning.

B: 1_____! The minibus was late picking me up.

A: When 2_____ set off?

B: Not until 9.30.

Dialogue 2

A: Come on, son. You're playing like you're half asleep!

B: 3_____, Boss. I'm really tired today.

A: When did you get to bed?

B: Ten o'clock. But I 4_____.

Dialogue 3

A: 5_____? I was completely unmarked!

B: Yeah, I know. Sorry 6_____.

A: Why didn't you pass when I shouted?

B: I thought I had a chance to score. 7_____, OK?

3 Practise reading the dialogues.

4 Make up similar dialogues for two of the following situations. For each one, apologize and give a reason.

a You missed a penalty (striker).

b You let in an easy goal (goalkeeper).

c You are very late meeting your friends.

d You forgot to do something important.

SKILLS SPOT

Holding the ball up

Brazilian players Ronaldo and Ronaldinho were geniuses on the football pitch. They could do anything with the ball, but they also did the basic things well. A striker often receives the ball with his back to goal and with no team-mate near him to receive a pass. In this situation the striker must use his body strength to keep the ball from the defender until he has a team-mate to pass to. This is called 'holding the ball up.'

Profile

Luis Suárez

English student and professional footballer

Date of birth:	24 January, 1987
Place of birth:	Salto, Uruguay
Height:	1.81 metres
Position:	Striker

Was it a big change for you to come and play in England?
Well, yes and no, because I had experience of European football at Ajax. It's not easy, but I think that top strikers have to score goals wherever they go!

Brazil and Argentina are traditionally the most successful teams in South America. Can Uruguay change that tradition?
Hey, Uruguay won the first ever World Cup! So history and tradition are on our side! Of course, Brazil and Argentina have a lot of quality players, but I think we have the same technique and ability as them.

Do South American teams enjoy attacking more than European teams?
Yes, I think so. Some teams have one forward who scores a lot of goals and other attacking players who create a lot. But when Uruguay won the Copa America in 2011, we had Diego Forlan, Edinson Cavani and me in the squad. We're three players who create and score a lot of goals!

Do you get frustrated if you don't score in a game?
Of course, I love to score goals. Obviously, if we win, I'm happy. But if we win and I've scored a goal, I'm happier!

It's often difficult to view footballers as normal people. What do you like to do when you're not playing football?
Probably the same as you! I like movies, music and visiting new places. But the most important thing for me is my family. Every goal that I score is for them.

Speaking   Discussion

1 Do you agree with these sentences?

1 There were more great strikers in the past.
2 South American strikers have more skill and technique than players from other parts of the world.
3 Young strikers can improve by watching video clips of great strikers from the past.
4 Great strikers score more than 20 goals every season.

Goalkeeper

Kick-off

1. Who is your favourite goalkeeper, and who does he play for? Why is he good?

2. Match the sentences with the pictures.

   1. He's taking a kick-out.
   2. He's collecting a cross.
   3. He's taking a goal kick.
   4. He's punching the ball clear.
   5. He's tipping the ball over the bar.
   6. He's making a save.

SKILLS SPOT ⚽

Narrowing the angles

Normally, in a one-on-one situation, the goalkeeper leaves the goal line to make it difficult for the attacking player to score a goal. When the goalkeeper moves out, he gives the attacking player less space to shoot at. He *narrows the angles*.

Reading

1 Do you play football video games? Which ones do you like? Why?

2 Read the text. What do you think is the best feature of the game?

A GREAT NEW GAME!

Danny, a video game designer, describes how he created the goalkeeper for his latest game.

I'm a bit different from other football game designers because I play a lot of football myself. I'm a goalkeeper, so for me it was important for the goalkeeper to be as realistic as possible. I watched DVDs of top-class keepers in action. I spoke to some real keepers, too. A lot of people gave us advice, and I think we have done a great job!

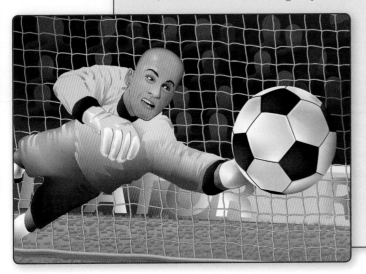

In this game, the keeper reacts differently in different situations. For simple shots he can catch it, and for shots that are going towards the top corner, he can tip the ball over the bar. The keeper can also use his body to make a block. I wanted the crosses to look realistic too, so the keeper can choose to come for the cross or stay on his goal line. When the keeper collects a cross or punches the ball, the supporters chant his name. But if he misses the cross, the fans boo him!

In real football, communication is very important for a keeper, especially during set-pieces. So in the game, you can record and upload ten different phrases for each player. So your keeper can shout instructions, like 'Switch on!' when you want the defenders to concentrate.

Finally, I'm especially pleased with the keeper's distribution. In a lot of football video games, the keeper just rolls the ball to the nearest player, or plays a long ball to the striker. Our goalkeeper has a lot more variety in his goal kicks, kick-outs, and throws. We worked hard on details like this, and I'm confident that the game will be a success.

3 Answer the questions.

1 How is Danny different from other game designers?
2 How did Danny prepare for the design of the game?
3 What happens if the goalkeeper makes a mistake during the game?
4 What can you upload?
5 Which part of the game is Danny especially happy with?

4 Match the verbs (1–5) with the definitions (a–e).

1 communicate   3 switch on   5 distribute
2 stay on your line   4 make a block

a throw, kick, or roll the ball to your team-mates in different parts of the pitch
b use words or signals to talk with your team-mates
c concentrate, especially when your team are defending
d remain on the goal line between the posts
e stop a goal with your body, without using your hands

Listening

FACTFILE

Name: Ben Amos
Date of birth: 10 April, 1990
Place of birth:
  Macclesfield, England
Height: 6ft 3in
Position: Goalkeeper

Did you know?

Ben is 6ft 3in tall. In the UK and USA we often measure height in feet and inches.
  1 foot = 30 cm
  1 inch = 2.5 cm

1 ⊙ 21   Listen and answer the questions about Ben.

1 Which part of training did Ben find difficult in the past?
2 What is the most important thing about training for Ben?
3 Why does Ben like his goalkeeping coach?
4 How did Edwin van der Sar help Ben?
5 Why doesn't Ben eat rice in the evening?
6 When did Ben discover that he enjoyed swimming?

2 What does the interviewer ask Ben? Complete the questions with *is* or *are* and the correct nouns from below.

team-mates   days off   goalkeeping coach   diet   training routine

1 Interviewer: What <u>*is your training routine*</u> like?
  Ben: Hard! We work with weights in the gym.
2 Interviewer: What _____ like?
  Ben: They're all good lads, and we get on.
3 Interviewer: What _____ like?
  Ben: I try to eat healthy food.
4 Interviewer: What _____ like?
  Ben: I don't get many, but they're great!

3 Make your own questions with *What … like?*

4 Match the terms (1–4) with the definitions (a–d). Look at the script of the interview on page 91 to help you.

1 core strength   a the speed you take to respond to something
2 high balls   b where the keeper stands in relation to the opposition
3 reactions   c to be strong in the middle of the body
4 positioning   d balls that the keeper has to jump for

Language

MAKE / DO

* Notice how Ben says: *you **make** a mistake* and *you **do** your best*
* We usually use *make* when we 'create' or 'build' something.
  I'm making a pizza.   *I'm going to make a cup of coffee.*

* We use ***do*** when we perform a more mechanical task. We often use ***do*** when we talk about work or jobs.
  I do exercises in the mornings.   *I have to do my homework tonight.*

* But with some phrases there is little reason why we use ***make*** or ***do***.
  *He **made** a good save.* **BUT** *He **did** a thorough warm up.*

Practice

1 Complete these sentences by choosing either *make* or *do*.

1 Ben *made*/ *did* a great save in training today!
2 Keepers *do* / *make* a lot of warm up exercises before the match.
3 Flamengo *did* / *made* a substitution at half time.
4 The goalie is *doing* / *making* a good job at organizing his defenders.
5 Real Madrid often *do* / *make* a big signing in the summer.

Reading

1 Read the text about Rogério Ceni and Luis Chilavert.

FOOTBALL LEGENDS:
CENI & CHILAVERT

CENI

Rogério Ceni and Luis Chilavert have a few things in common. They are South American. They have had long careers. They have been team captains. And, perhaps most incredibly of all, they are goalkeepers who have scored lots of goals! Their goals have come from penalties or free-kicks.

They were born and grew up 600 km apart. Ceni is from Pato Branco in Brazil, while Chilavert is from Luque in Paraguay. Chilavert has scored over 60 professional goals in his career, while Ceni has scored more than 100 professional goals in over 1,000 appearances for São Paulo!

CHILAVERT

At international level, Ceni has been to two World Cups, 2002 and 2006. But he wasn't first-choice keeper for Brazil during these competitions, and ended up with a total of only ten minutes on the pitch. On the other hand, Chilavert played for Paraguay at the 1998 and 2002 World Cups, and did quite well. He took the free-kicks for his team, and almost scored against Spain.

Ceni has never scored for Brazil, but Chilavert has scored 8 international goals in 74 appearances for his country.

2 Read the statements below. Are they True (**T**) or False (**F**)?

1 Ceni and Chilavert have been captains of their teams. ___

2 Ceni has played more than 1,000 games. ___

3 Both players have played in a World Cup. ___

4 All their goals have been penalties. ___

5 Chilavert has scored in a World Cup. ___

3 Have you ever seen a goalkeeper score a goal? Describe it.

Language

PRESENT PERFECT: *HAVE / HAS* + PAST PARTICIPLE

Affirmative
I've played in goal.
He's played in goal.

Negative
I haven't played in goal.
He hasn't played in goal.

- We can use the Present Perfect to talk about an experience from the past. It is not important when it happened.

- Compare the two sentences.
  I **played** in the 2002 World Cup.   I have **played** in three World Cups.

- In the first sentence we know when the event happened, so we use the Past Simple. In the second sentence the time is not specified, so we use the Present Perfect.

Practice

1 Complete using the Present Perfect form of the verb.

1 Ceni _has played_ over 1,000 games for São Paolo. (play)

2 I _____ 20 goals this season. (score)

3 Brazil _____ the World Cup five times. (win)

4 We _____ training yet. (not finish)

2 Past Simple or Present Perfect? Circle the correct verb form.

1 Pelé *scored* / *has scored* a hat-trick in the World Cup in 1958.

2 I *supported* / *have supported* my local team for the last ten years.

3 Yesterday we *had* / *have had* a double training session.

4 Júlio César *made* / *has made* a fantastic save from Lionel Messi in the Champions League in 2010.

Listening

1 ⊙ 22 Listen to three extracts about goalkeeper injuries. Which player injured himself off the field?

2 Listen again and complete the table.

	Bert Trautmann	Santiago Cañizares	Petr Čech
Nationality			Czech
Year of injury	1956		
Part of the body injured			

3 Complete these other injuries using the words below.

ankle	broken	muscle
torn	bruised a bone	shoulder

1 I've _bruised a bone_ in my foot.

2 I've pulled a _____.

3 I've _____ my hamstring.

4 I've dislocated my _____.

5 I've sprained my _____.

6 I've _____ my leg.

4 Ask and answer questions using *Have you ever ...?*

Have you ever pulled a muscle? Yes, I have. / No, I haven't.

Did you know?

When people are in good physical condition we say they are *fit*. *Fit* is also the opposite of *injured*. *He's injured at the moment, but he'll be fit to play again next month.*

Reading **1** Does your country have many good goalkeepers? Read this article about Spanish goalkeepers.

SPANISH KEEPERS

I'm a Spanish supporter and, in Spain, our goalkeeping situation has become a big problem. For some countries, it's difficult to find even one good goalkeeper. For a few years, we have had too many to choose from!

Iker Casillas, Pepe Reina, David de Gea and Víctor Valdés have all played club football for some of the biggest teams in the world. But of course, only one can play for the national team. So, since 2010, the other three keepers have had to fight for a place on the bench.

All four goalkeepers are excellent in every department: positioning, commanding the penalty area, organizing the defence, distribution and, of course, they are great **shot-stoppers**[1]. I have seen all of these players make **match-winning saves**[2] in important games. I remember when de Gea saved a Diego Milito penalty in the European Super Cup!

And if our **first-choice keeper**[3] is injured, the substitutes are so good that nobody worries. It's difficult to choose a favourite, but I have two. David de Gea, because his reactions are so good, and Pepe Reina, because he can create a goal from nothing with a **long ball**[4].

2 Answer the questions.

1 What is Spain's goalkeeping problem?

2 Which keepers are the writer's favourites?

3 Which keeper has great reactions?

4 What are the five 'departments' of goalkeeping?

3 Match the terms in bold in the text with the definitions below.

a ball played from one end of the pitch to the other

b important saves a keeper makes to ensure his team win a game

c name often given to goalkeepers who can make good saves

d keeper that the manager picks to start every game

Language

> ## FOR / SINCE
>
> - *For* and *since* are often used with the Present Perfect tense.
> - We use *for* with a period of time that continues into the present.
>   *I've lived here for four years.*   *He hasn't scored a goal for five games.*
> - We use *since* when we say the time when the period began.
>   *He hasn't played in goal since he was 15 years old.*

Practice **1** Choose *for* or *since*.

1 Reina has saved a lot of penalties *for* / *since* the start of his career.

2 Valdés has won many trophies *for* / *since* he started playing football.

3 Casillas has been Spain's top keeper *for* / *since* ten years.

4 De Gea has played professional football *for* / *since* 2009.

Everyday English Helping others

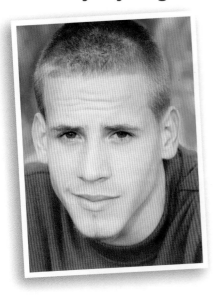

1 ⊙ 23 Listen to Karsten in three situations. What are the people offering to do each time?

2 Listen again and complete the dialogues.

Dialogue 1

A: Hi Karsten. Where are you going?

B: The airport. I'm ¹_____ for the Germany Under-17s!

A: That's the best news I've had all day! Well done!

B: Thanks!

A: How are you getting there? ²_____ a lift?

B: I've ordered a taxi actually.

A: Come on, ³_____ take you.

Dialogue 2

A: ⁴_____, Karsten?

B: I've hurt my shoulder, Doc.

A: ⁵_____ at it, OK? How did it happen exactly?

B: I fell on my shoulder when I went for a header.

A: ⁶_____ any painkillers or physio?

B: Just some gel, but it's really painful.

A: Right, I'll give you something for it.

Dialogue 3

A: Right lads, who's going to help me take this equipment outside?

B: I'll ⁷_____, Coach!

A: I thought you were injured, Karsten.

B: I was, but I've had physio. My shoulder's fine now, so I'm fit to play!

A: Great stuff! ⁸_____ – carry this!

SKILLS SPOT ⚽

Saving a penalty

1 Try to see if the penalty-taker looks to a particular side of the goal as he places the ball.

2 The front foot of the penalty-taker often points in the direction the taker wants the ball to go.

3 Never dive before the ball is kicked.

4 Dive towards the ball, as well as to your chosen side. This narrows the angle for the penalty-taker.

5 A player who takes a fast run-up doesn't usually side-foot the ball. So if he's right-footed he will probably kick it to your right.

Profile

David de Gea

English student and professional footballer

Date of birth: **7 November, 1990**

Place of birth: **Madrid, Spain**

Height: **1.91 metres**

Position: **Goalkeeper**

How have you adapted to life in England?

Well, I've had some difficulties – that's normal – but I've adapted OK. I've found a good place to live which is important, because I'm a quiet person and I like to be at home. Also, my parents have been here with me, and a lot of people have helped me. I've even had a friendly taxi-driver who tries to speak Spanish with me!

Have you enjoyed learning the language?

I've enjoyed my lessons, yes. I'm a bit shy, but I've tried to practise with the other players and some of the staff. It's hard work, but it's been fun!

In what ways has training been different?

Oh, training has been very different! I've done a lot more strength work here, and not only with weights. Also, here you have to perform in training every day – like in a game. You can't see the manager, but you know he's watched the training session from his window!

What has surprised you about your career?

It's incredible how my life has changed very quickly. My life changed when I got into the first team at Atlético Madrid, and now I'm a Manchester United player! Unbelievable! It's been fantastic to work with Sir Alex Ferguson and Eric Steele.

Have you ever given yourself 10/10 after a game?

Keepers are perfectionists … I've had some good performances in big games, but I've never had a perfect game!

Speaking Discussion

1 Do you agree with these statements?

1 Goalkeeper has always been a boring position.

2 Goalkeepers work harder than other players.

3 It's easier to be a goalkeeper in a hot country than in a country with a cold climate.

4 It's better to play every week for a small team than to sit on the bench for a big team.

Scout

Kick-off

1 Who are the players? Match the descriptions (1–4) to the players (A–D).

1 He's thin and he's got long, dark hair.

2 He's stocky and he's bald.

3 He's very tall and athletic.

4 He's tall and he's got short, fair hair.

2 These words and phrases are used to describe physical appearance. Match the opposites.

1 short   2 stocky   3 dark hair   4 long hair   5 straight hair

a fair hair   b tall   c short hair   d curly hair   e slim

3 These words are used to describe a player's skills or personality. Match the words that have similar meanings.

1 fast   2 clever   3 skilful   4 brave   5 strong

a smart   b tough   c quick   d courageous   e technical

4 Put the descriptions with the correct question.

He's medium height.   He's stocky.   He's a good leader.
He's got long, curly hair.   He's brave.

What's Carles Puyol like?	What does Carles Puyol look like?

5 Write three short descriptions of famous players. Include their physical appearance and their skills or personality.

Reading   **1**   Read and answer the quiz questions.

QUIZ TIME

1 Who is the oldest goalscorer in the history of the World Cup?

2 What is the biggest stadium in England?

3 Who became the most expensive player in the world when he joined Real Madrid in 2009?

4 Only one Premier League team has a bigger pitch than Manchester United. Which is it?

5 Which country is the most successful in the history of the World Cup?

6 Which English team has been more successful in the European Cup than in its domestic league?

Language

COMPARATIVES AND SUPERLATIVES

		Comparative	Superlative
Short adjectives	fast	faster	fastest
	strong	stronger	strongest
Long adjectives	expensive	more expensive	most expensive
	successful	more successful	most successful
Irregular adjectives	good	better	best
	bad	worse	worst

*Wingers are often **faster than** other players.*
*Gareth Bale is one of **the fastest** players in the Premier League.*

Practice   **1**   Read the conversations between a scout and a manager. Complete using the phrases below.

faster than   older than   more expensive than   the fastest

Conversation 1

A: How old is the centre-back? 16?

B: No, I think he's ¹_____ that, Boss.

Conversation 2

A: Which player will you sign? João or Paulinho?

B: Well, João's a great player, but he's ²_____ Paulinho.

Conversation 3

A: Is the right back fast?

B: Yes, he is, and he is ³_____ the left-back.

A: Is he ⁴_____ player in the team?

B: Yes, he is.

2 Look at the players on page 46. Write sentences to compare the players using the adjectives below.

tall   skilful   short   athletic   tough   fast

Clarence Seedorf is shorter than Emmanuel Adebayor.

Listening

1 Read about the discovery of George Best. Can you explain the last sentence?

In 1961, Manchester United scout Bob Bishop saw a 15-year-old playing in Northern Ireland. His name was George Best. Bob Bishop sent a message to the manager, Matt Busby, saying, 'I think I've found you a genius!' Best helped United to win the 1968 European Cup, and Pelé described Best as 'the greatest player of all time'. There is a saying in Northern Ireland: 'Maradona good, Pelé better, George Best.'

2 ⊙ 24 Listen to three scouts. Complete the table.

	Steve	Peter	Richard
Number of years in the job	_____	_____	_____
Most important thing about the job	not to waste the _____	to discover _____ before the big clubs	to _____ everything down
Quality I look for in a player	_____	_____	_____ ability
Most expensive signing	_____	_____	none
Best moment as a scout	when I didn't sign a bad player	when a player _____ debut	when we _____ _____

3 Look at two sentences that Peter says. Complete the sentences below using the correct form of *remember* or *remind*.

I _remember_ when I first saw him.   He _reminds_ me of Johan Cruijff.

1 The scout says that I _____ him of Gianluigi Buffon.

2 I can't _____ where I put my kit bag. Have you seen it?

3 Can you _____ me to ask for new shin pads at training?

4 Do you _____ your first pair of football boots?

SKILLS SPOT ⚽
....
Cruijff turn
This move was famously performed by Dutch legend Johan Cruijff.

1 Cut inside so the defender thinks you want to play the ball across him.

2 When the defender tries to block it, use your foot to pull the ball behind you.

3 Change direction and follow the ball, leaving the defender behind!

Reading

1 Read the article about a scout. Match the paragraphs (1–6) with the pictures (A–F) below.

The secrets of scouting

Liverpool FC scout, Frank McParland, has a lot of experience finding new players. Here he gives us a guide to what he looks for in players in each position.

A goalkeeper

B full-back

D centre-back

C central midfielder

E striker

F winger

1 When I'm looking for a _____, I want a player who can dribble and beat defenders. He must be good at crossing, and he has to have enough pace to track back after an attack **breaks down[1]**.

2 _____ is a very important position for me. Somebody in this position has to be good in the air, and at **organizing[2]** the players around him. He doesn't have to be very fast if he has good positioning sense. He must be brave, and good at tackling.

3 A good _____ should have excellent marking ability. Pace is also important. If he is going forward to support attacks, he needs to be able to get back into position quickly. He should also be able to tackle well with both feet, in case the player he's marking cuts inside.

4 I always look for a _____ who has good **reflexes[3]**. He should be quite tall, although he doesn't have to be a giant! He has to control the penalty area and, ultimately, he has to be trusted by his defence.

5 A very good _____ is perhaps the hardest thing to find. He should be fast, of course, but he must also be clever, like a fox! A defender can just head the ball anywhere but this guy has to be very **accurate[4]** with the direction of his headers. If he is composed and calm, this will help him when he's finishing.

6 I like a _____ who can dictate the **rhythm[5]** of the game. It's important that he doesn't always go for the 'spectacular' pass. It's more important that he **keeps possession[6]** until the time is right to make the final ball. He also has to be able to tackle, but pace is not so important in this position.

2 Match the terms in bold in the text with the words or phrases below.

a precise   c instructing   e reactions
b tempo   d comes to an end / stops   f be in control of the ball

3 For each position, choose a player of your own and describe his qualities.

Language

> ## MUST / HAVE TO / SHOULD
>
> - We use *must* and *have to* when it is necessary to do something.
>   *He's a wonderful player. We **must** sign him!*
>   *He **has to** improve his fitness if he wants to play in this league.*
>   - For the past of *have to* and *must*, we use *had to*.
>   *When he was a boy, Ronaldo **had** to borrow a pair of football boots.*
> - Be careful! Although *must* and *have to* are similar in affirmative sentences, they have very different meanings in negative sentences.
>   - We use *mustn't* when something is not allowed.
>   *A goalkeeper **mustn't** pick up the ball if a player passes it to him.*
>   - We use *don't have to* when something is not necessary.
>   *Players **don't have to** kick the ball out of play when a player is injured.*
> - We use *should* when something is advisable but not necessary.
>   *I think you **should** speak to the doctor about your back.*

Practice

1 Circle the correct verb.

1 I don't think you *must /* *should* celebrate in front of the other team's fans.

2 Scouts *mustn't / don't have to* be ex-players, but it helps if they are.

3 During a direct free kick, opposition players *have to / should* stand at least 9.15 metres from the ball.

4 I think he's injured. Maybe we *must / should* take him off.

5 Coaches *mustn't / don't have to* go on the pitch during a match.

6 Which club do you think I *have to / should* join?

7 You *mustn't / shouldn't* forget how important it is to rest in your free time.

2 What are the people saying? Match the sentences with the pictures, and complete using the correct form of *must*, *have to* or *should*.

1 Sorry I'm late! I _____ wait for the bus.

2 If the boss wants to win, he _____ bring me on.

3 Do you _____ see the physio every day?

4 You _____ drink that before a match.

5 You _____ walk on the pitch!

Listening

1 ⊙ 25 James is a scout. Listen to him speaking to his manager.

2 Listen again and answer the questions.

1 What position is James's player?

2 How does James think he will improve the team?

3 If he signs the player, what will the manager have to do?

Language

FUTURE: *WILL*

• We often use *will* or *won't* for predictions.

*I'm sure our scouts **will** discover the next Rooney!*
*They **won't** qualify for the Copa Libertadores this season.*

Practice

1 Listen again. Use *will* or *won't* and a verb to complete each sentence.

1 He _____ ten goals a season.

2 He _____ us more options.

3 He _____ any problems with the language.

2 Ask and answer the questions. Think of more questions.

1 Who do you think will win the next World Cup?

2 Which team will win the Champions League this year?

3 Who will win the FIFA Ballon d'Or this season?

Language

FIRST CONDITIONAL: *IF* + PRESENT + FUTURE

• We use the first conditional to talk about a situation in the present and its probable result.

*If we **sign** him, **he'll** score ten goals a season.*
*If you **don't train** hard, **you'll never play** for the first team.*

Practice

1 Complete the sentences using the correct form of the verb.

1 If you _____ well, you'll have fewer injuries. (eat)

2 You'll never play in midfield if you _____ possession all the time. (lose)

3 If you pass the ball more, you _____ more friends in the team! (have)

4 Jean-Claude _____, if he's fit. (play)

2 You are a scout. Think about a player you know. What would you say about him to the manager? Consider the questions below.

Is he smart/ tough/skilful?

Is he good at marking/tackling?

Is he good in the air?

Is he good at crossing/ heading/passing the ball?

Does he have good pace/reflexes?

Has he got a good shot?

Can he take accurate penalties/free-kicks?

How will he improve?

Everyday English

Asking for and giving advice

We often use *should* to give advice in English, but there are many other expressions that we can use to do this.

1 ⊙ 26 Listen to the three dialogues. What advice is being given each time?

2 Listen again and complete the dialogues.

Dialogue 1

A: So, now that I'm in the youth team, what [1]_____ I do to improve as a player?

B: Well, you [2]_____ to understand more about your position – and make yourself as strong as the other lads.

A: Do I have to do weights? [3]_____?

B: No, [4]_____ do weights yet. You're still too young.

Dialogue 2

A: [5]_____ about signing him?

B: He's a decent player, Boss, and he's got a great first touch – but he's small, and I don't know if he'll grow much more.

A: [6]_____ speak to the other scouts?

Dialogue 3

A: What's up, Alberto?

B: There are scouts at the game today. I'm nervous! [7]_____?

A: You don't have to worry about that, son. [8]_____ you take it easy for the first ten minutes, and then show them what you can do.

3 Practise reading the dialogues.

4 Make up dialogues for two of the following situations.

1 You have a headache after training.

2 Your team-mate is always diving.

3 You need to lose five kilograms.

4 Your friend wants to save up some money.

SKILLS SPOT

First touch

When the ball is passed to you, it's important to control it. A good *first touch* gives you possession of the ball, and time to decide what you want to do with it. Many scouts pay a lot of attention to a player's first touch.

Profile

Javier Hernández

English student and professional footballer

Date of birth: **1 June, 1988**

Place of birth: **Guadalajara, Mexico**

Height: **1.75 metres**

Position: **Striker**

Can you tell us about signing for Manchester United?

There were times when I thought about quitting football to concentrate on my studies. So when my dad told me that Jim Lawlor, Manchester United's chief scout, wanted to talk to me, I couldn't believe it!

What happened next?

Jim spoke to the Chivas president and I flew to England with my dad. We watched the Champions League game against Bayern Munich at Old Trafford, and had lunch with Sir Alex Ferguson the next day. All this had to be top secret!

Then you played for both sides when United played at Chivas, and you even scored for your old club …

Yes, that was a very emotional day! It was the first game at Chivas' new stadium. In the end, United lost 3-2, but I started for Chivas, and switched teams at half-time! I will always remember it.

You had a dream first season. You won the Premier League and scored 20 goals …

Yes, but when I first arrived, and I saw how physical the game was here, I remember thinking to myself, 'Will I ever get off the bench?' But gradually, I started to get more chances.

Your English is very good. Has that helped you?

Thank you! I hope it will continue to improve. It has helped. It was useful to be able to speak to Jim, and then to Sir Alex and my team-mates from the beginning. If you live in another country, you have to try and learn the language. It's the minimum you can do.

Speaking Discussion

1 Do you agree with these sentences?

1 Anyone can be a scout. Great players are easy to identify.

2 Clubs can save a lot of money by scouting young players.

3 If a scout doesn't discover you by the age of sixteen, you will never play in the top leagues.

4 European scouts think that all players have to be able to defend.

Manager

Kick-off

1 Who are the best managers at the moment? What does a manager do?

2 Match the pictures (A–F) with the sentences below (1–6).

A

B

C

D

E

F

1 He's celebrating a goal.

2 He's signing a new player.

3 He's giving a press conference.

4 He's giving advice.

5 He's coaching the team.

6 He's making a substitution.

SKILLS SPOT ⚽

Man-management

If a player isn't playing regularly, or if he is having problems off the pitch, he can lose his motivation. Sometimes he doesn't play as well as he can. Good managers know how to help their players. Often this is by making them feel important to the team.

Listening

1 Match the manager's instructions (1–4) with the pictures (A–D).

1 Tackle him! 2 Shoot! 3 Concentrate! 4 Give it to Stephen!

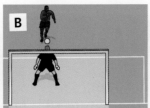

2 ⊙ 27 Listen to a manager speaking to his players before a game. Complete the table.

Player	Starting position	Instruction
Kristian		_____ the space behind him.
Tyrone		_____ the target!
Daniel		_____ me.
Chakri		_____ the ball on the ground.
Farooq	substitute	_____ ready!

Language

IMPERATIVES

We use imperatives to give instructions or advice.

- Affirmative imperatives have the same form as the infinitive without *to*.

  Warm up!   ***Look up*** *before you cross!*

- Negative imperatives have *do not (don't)* + infinitive.

  Don't give *the ball away!*   ***Don't foul*** *him!*

Practice

1 ⊙ 28 Listen to the manager's instructions. Complete the sentences using the imperatives below.

keep going   don't give the ball away   shoot
give it to him   now get back into position

1 Stephen's free! _____!

2 Great tackle, Paul! _____!

3 Marco, _____!

4 That's good, Kai! _____!

5 _____! Oh, that was close. Good effort!

2 Match the situations (1–5) with the instructions (a–e).

1 The striker's standing beside the centre-back, waiting for a through-ball.

2 The second keeper is sitting on the bench when the first keeper gets injured.

3 The centre-back's waiting for an opposition corner to be taken.

4 The right-back's playing too many long, high balls up to his striker.

5 The midfielder's taking a free-kick in the last minute of the match.

a Warm up!

b Keep the ball on the ground!

Stay onside!

d Hit the target!

e Don't
se your man!

55

Reading 1 Iñaki was in charge of teams in both England and Spain. Read about his different jobs.

COACH OR MANAGER?

Friends often ask me why I was a coach in Spain, but a manager in England. The answer is that while all managers are coaches, not all coaches are managers!

COACH

In Spain, I arrived at the training ground every morning and I coached the team. After the training sessions I prepared the team for the next game. I showed the players videos of our next opponents and discussed the tactics and formation I wanted to use. We also reviewed our previous game, and talked about how we could improve. I enjoyed advising key players on things like their positional play. Every weekend, I picked the team, gave the team-talk, and after the game I gave a press conference.

In Spain, the club president normally makes decisions on signing players. Once a president sent me an email to ask my opinion of a player he was going to sign. I told him, 'Don't sign that player! He is a bad influence in the dressing room.' The next morning, on my way to training, I heard on the radio that we were signing the player!

MANAGER

After three successful seasons in Spain, I went to England and became a manager. I soon discovered that it was a 24-hour-a-day job. On the first day, the chairman said, 'Tell me which players you're going to sell, and which players you're going to buy!' Instead of working with the players, I spent most of my first two weeks meeting with scouts and players' agents. In Spain, the president and the club's general manager did this type of work.

In England I had several coaches who helped me prepare the team for games, and who normally led the training sessions. But it was my job to select the starting 11. I also spoke with the media, and did press conferences.

As manager I didn't have enough time to work with individual players. Instead I worked with the players as a group every day. I had meetings all the time: at the club academy; with our scouts; with the chairman; and with all of the other coaches at the club, even at schoolboy level.

I prefer working directly with players. So at the end of the season I returned to Spain.

2 What were Iñaki's responsibilities as a coach and a manager? Complete the table by putting either a tick (✔) or a cross (✗).

	Coach	Manager
Preparing the team for games		✔
Picking the team		
Giving press conferences		
Signing players		
Meeting players' agents		
Helping individual players to improve		

Did you know? ⚽

Some managers use a *squad rotation* system to rest players and to give other players a chance, instead of playing the same team in every game.

3 Think about a manager or coach you know. What does he do at the club?

Listening

1 Read about a manager called Nathan.

Nathan's team won their league last year, so they've been promoted this season. It won't be easy in the top division, but they hope to stay up. Now they've got a new owner, and a lot more money to spend. Nathan's decided to make some changes at the club.

2 What kinds of changes do clubs make when they are promoted?

3 ⊚ 29 Listen to Nathan. Are the sentences True (**T**) or False (**F**)?

1 Nathan's team are going to be more defensive this season. _____

2 Nathan's going to buy a new striker. _____

3 He's going to improve the academy training ground. _____

4 He's going to change the coaching staff. _____

5 He's going to improve transport to away games. _____

Language

GOING TO

- When we intend or plan to do something, we use *going to*.

  *We're **going to practise** set-pieces today.*   *I'm **going to sign** him.*

- We also use *going to* when we expect something to happen in the future.

  *It's **going to be** a difficult game.*
  *He's not **going to win** anything with this team.*

Practice

1 What is the manager going to do? Complete the sentences.

speak   sign   watch   give

Tomorrow...

1 I'm going to _____ a new player.

2 I'm going to _____ a press conference.

3 I'm going to _____ a DVD with the team.

4 I'm going to _____ to the physio.

2 Complete the sentences. Use *going to* with the verbs below.

save   be   win   celebrate   speak

1 His back's hurting. He's _____ to the physio.

2 It's the manager's birthday tomorrow. We're _____ the game for him.

3 It's a great shot! The keeper's not _____ it!

4 Drink lots of water before the game. It's _____ very hot today.

5 We're champions! The fans are _____ tonight.

Reading

1 Spanish coach Rodolfo Borrell has coached at FC Barcelona and Liverpool FC. Read his instructions on ways to beat the keeper.

2 Match the descriptions with the pictures.

HOW TO BEAT THE KEEPER

1 You kick the ball with the outside of your foot. It's difficult for the keeper to save because of the way the ball moves in the air. If you're left-footed, the ball curves from right to left when you do this. The famous left-footed player Roberto Carlos scored a fantastic goal for Brazil against France with this type of shot from a free-kick.

2 It's best to try this type of shot when the keeper is off his line. The ball starts on the ground and you lean forward when you kick the ball. You try to get your foot under the ball as much as possible. The ball normally goes high and, if you're good at it, it drops over the keeper's head and into the goal.

3 For this type of shot, the ball must be in the air and the keeper must be off his line. You kick the ball over the goalkeeper's head. It's best to side-foot the ball to get the most control on your shot. You don't get the opportunity to score a goal like this very often.

4 This type of shot is used a lot by free-kick specialists. In the past, David Beckham was famous for his ability to shoot from free-kicks using this type of shot. You kick the ball with the inside of your foot and it is very effective for getting the ball around the defensive wall when you're taking a free-kick.

Reading

1 Every manager needs a goalkeeping coach. What do you know about this job?

2 Eric Steele has coached top keepers Peter Schmeichel, and Edwin van der Sar. Read what Eric says about the job.

Goalkeeping coach

Training sessions

When I'm planning training sessions, I always start with the game in mind, and work back from that. I want to be clear about the keeper's frame of mind the day before the game. Actually, I prefer not to talk too much on the day of the game. And for away games there's a lot more preparation, especially if the keeper has no experience of playing at a particular ground, in a particular atmosphere. You need a degree of variety, so I like to use DVDs and computers when I'm explaining tactics. Most importantly, you need to be flexible. That means you have to be able to listen to the keepers and ask them, 'What do you need?'

Competition

Having competition among your keepers is also very important. Keeper number three has to understand that at any minute, he can become keeper number two. This happens when there's an injury for instance. Suddenly he's on the bench with a chance of becoming number one! I always tell the lads that their job demands them to be available to give their best, 365 days of the year. And they have to be able to work together. Generally, there's great solidarity. The attitude is this: 'We support each other, but we compete!'

Responsibilities

The main responsibility is to give the manager options. My job is to prepare the keeper in four areas: technical, tactical, physical and mental. That means I take a lot of interest in what the keeper is eating, how focused he is in the gym, and above all, how he's feeling!

3 Eric prepares keepers in four areas. Match the areas (1–4) with the descriptions (a–d).

1 technical	a	condition of player's body
2 tactical	b	player's skill or ability to perform his job
3 physical	c	player's confidence and strength of mind
4 mental	d	player's understanding of the game, and his team's game-plan

4 Read. Are the sentences True (**T**) or False (**F**)?

1 Eric selects the keeper who starts the game. _____

2 Eric doesn't say much to the keeper on the day of a game. _____

3 Eric's role for home and away games doesn't change. _____

4 Eric always wants to hear the keepers' opinions. _____

5 ◉ 30 Listen and answer the questions.

1 Did Eric play at the same level as Schmeichel and van der Sar?

2 What did Eric say to van der Sar?

3 How did Schmeichel and van der Sar react to Eric's questions?

4 What can make a top keeper angry in training?

Everyday English Expressing quantity

1 ⊚ 31 Listen to the three dialogues. What are the people talking about each time?

2 Listen again and complete the dialogues.

Dialogue 1

A: ¹_____ pasta have you got on your plate?

B: Just ²_____, Boss. Why?

A: Because you're ³_____, son! And you've got too much bread there! One slice ⁴_____ .

B: But I'm going to have another training session this afternoon.

A: I know that, but look what the keeper's eating, and he's ⁵_____ than you!

Dialogue 2

A: Not ⁶_____, lad!

B: But I've had ⁷_____ balls to feet, Boss.

A: Come on, Karl! You've had ⁸_____ anybody else. ⁹_____ opportunities do you need before you score?

B: Sorry, Boss, but they're marking me out of the game!

A: Well, I've ¹⁰_____ for today. I'm going to take you off for the second half. ¹¹_____ did we pay for you?

Dialogue 3

A: Great work, Karl! ¹²_____!

B: Thanks, Boss! I got ¹³_____ for the second goal.

A: You make your own luck, son. You were ¹⁴_____ for them.

B: Am I going to play ¹⁵_____ now, Boss?

A: Well, you've created ¹⁶_____ for their defence today, and you've got a couple of good goals. ¹⁷_____ are you going to score for us this season?

SKILLS SPOT ⚽

Protecting a lead

When his team are winning a game, a manager often makes a tactical change to *protect the lead*. This usually involves taking off an attacking player and replacing him with a more defensive substitute. The manager of a team playing in a 4-4-2 formation will often take off one of his strikers and replace him with a defensive midfielder or defender, and change to a 4-5-1 formation.

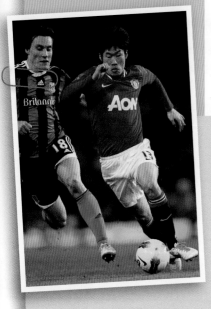

Profile

Park Ji-Sung
English student and professional footballer

Date of birth: **25 February, 1981**

Place of birth: **Goheung, South Korea**

Height: **1.77 metres**

Position: **Midfielder**

You've been described as a 'manager's dream' because of your fitness levels! Are you a typical Asian footballer?

Asia's so big and so varied that you can't talk about a typical Asian player. It's true that in South Korea, we learn to do what the coaches ask us to do, so perhaps that discipline is typical of South Koreans …

Can you see an Asian team winning the World Cup?

Anything can happen in a tournament, but it's difficult … it's so hard to win the World Cup! In 2002, we reached the semi-finals, and thanks to our coach, the spirit of the players, the enthusiasm of the fans, and a bit of luck, we did far better than we could have imagined. But winning is totally different! Many things have to come together at the same time. Think about England; there's such a strong football culture here, and a lot of top-level players, but they haven't won since 1966!

You've played for two great managers, Guus Hiddink and Sir Alex Ferguson. What's so special about them?

They're both incredible managers who not only have the ability to make the right selection in terms of the starting 11, but who can successfully manage a big group of more than 20 players and keep the whole squad happy. They know when and how to talk to everyone and make them feel important. All the boys want to play, but even if they don't play all the time, these managers give them confidence and belief so that they are motivated to train. When their chance comes, they're ready!

Would you like to be a coach or a manager in the future?

Absolutely not! I'm not the right kind of person. You have to be able to handle incredible pressure. It's so stressful – a 24-hour-a-day job!

Speaking Discussion

1 Do you agree with these sentences?

1 The manager is the most important person at a club.

2 Many top clubs don't give the manager enough time in the job.

3 It's important for players to be afraid of their manager.

4 In the future, more managers are going to come from outside the sport.

The greatest

Kick-off

1 Who do you think are the greatest players of all time?

2 Look at this dream team. Do you agree with the choices? Can you think of three players to complete it?

Gianluigi Buffon
Cafu
Roberto Carlos
?
Franz Beckenbauer
?
Zinedine Zidane
Ryan Giggs
Pelé
Ronaldo
?

3 Read the descriptions of the three missing players and choose them from the photos below.

1 He's tall, muscular, fast, and skilful.
2 He's stocky with long curly hair, and he's creative.
3 He's quite short for his position, with short hair and blue eyes.

4 Select your own team to play against the *dream team*. Think of reasons to explain your choices.

I've chosen Clarence Seedorf to play in midfield because he's strong, very clever, and he's got a fantastic shot.

5 How much do you think your team would cost? Do you think that good players cost too much today?

Reading

1 Do you think managers need to be successful ex-players?

2 Read about the manager of the great AC Milan team of 1989.

ARRIGO SACCHI

Managers such as José Mourinho and Arrigo Sacchi have shown that you don't need to have much experience as a player to reach the top as a manager.

Sacchi never played professionally. In fact, he worked as a shoe salesman! But when people said he didn't have enough experience to be a manager, Sacchi famously answered, 'I didn't know you had to be a horse before you could become a jockey'!

He took Italy to the World Cup Final in 1994, but people remember him more for his fantastic AC Milan team. In fact, with AC Milan, he became the only manager to have back-to-back wins in the European Cup (today's Champions League) in 1989 and 1990. The same team also won the Italian league title in 1988, the European Super Cup in 1989 and 1990, and the Intercontinental Cup (today's Club World Cup) also in 1989 and 1990.

A lot of people at the time said there were too many foreigners in the AC Milan team. This is perhaps hard for us to understand, especially because they only had three non-Italian regular starters: the wonderful Dutch trio of Marco van Basten, Frank Rijkaard, and Ruud Gullit.

Today's teams are so international that José Mourinho's Inter won the Champions League Final in 2010 with not a single Italian in the starting line-up. And there weren't too many Inter fans who complained!

Sacchi is famous for his system of pressing and zonal marking. He says that a great team is one 'in which players are connected to each other, which moves together, as if it were a single player'. Just like his famous Milan team! Many people believe they were the strongest club side of all time – even better than the Barcelona team of recent years.

3 Answer the questions.

　　1 What was Sacchi's job before he became a manager?

　　2 How far did Sacchi's Italy side go in the 1994 World Cup?

　　3 What nationality were Sacchi's foreign players at AC Milan?

4 Which do you think is the greatest team ever? Explain your choice.

SKILLS SPOT ⚽

Zonal marking

Zonal marking is a defensive system in which each defender covers an area of the pitch, not a particular opponent. When the team win possession, the players are in position to attack more quickly. AC Milan had a lot of success playing this system in the late 1980s.

Language

MANY / MUCH / TOO / ENOUGH

- *Many* is used for plural nouns.

  Many *people think Arrigo Sacchi's Milan were the strongest club side ever.*

- *Much* is used for uncountable nouns.

  *Sacchi showed that you don't need to have **much** experience as a player.*

- *Too many / much* means more than you need or want.

  *There were **too many** foreign players in the team.*

- *Enough* means fully adequate in quantity.

  *He didn't have **enough** experience.*

Practice

1 Complete the sentences with the work below.

much   too   too many   too much   enough

1 For 60 games, nobody could beat José Mourinho's Chelsea at Stamford Bridge. They were _____ strong.

2 People said Mourinho wasn't experienced _____, but he's been a great manager at four different clubs.

3 In April 2011, Mourinho dropped Ronaldo for talking _____ about team tactics.

4 How _____ does Mourinho get paid?

5 I can't remember all the trophies that Mourinho's won! There are _____!

Listening

1 ⊙ 32 Listen to four supporters discussing which players and teams they think are the greatest. Which player is mentioned twice?

2 Listen again and complete the table.

	Greatest current team	Greatest team of all time	Greatest current player	Greatest player of all time	Greatest goal
Frank	_____	Brazil 1970	_____	George Best	Wayne Rooney v. Manchester City
Beatriz	Real Madrid	_____	_____	_____	Clarence Seedorf v. Atlético Madrid
Marco	_____	_____	David Silva	_____	Marco van Basten v. Russia
Cristina	_____	Ajax 1971	_____	Johan Cruijff	_____ _____

Reading

1 Do you ever consider defenders when you talk about the best players in the world?

2 Read about Franz Beckenbauer. What is his unique record?

THE GREATEST DEFENDER

The first defender to appear in the FIFA World Player of the Year top three was Paolo Maldini who came second in 1995. Another Italian legend, Fabio Cannavaro, went one better when he won the award in 2006. However, many people think the greatest defender of all time was Franz Beckenbauer of Germany.

Beckenbauer played in a defensive position known as 'sweeper' or 'libero'. This position hasn't been very popular recently, but a sweeper plays between the two centre-backs. In fact, Beckenbauer's job was to play as a fifth defender, to break up opposition attacks, and then get forward to start attacks for his own team.

In Beckenbauer's first season with Bayern Munich in 1964, they got promoted to the Bundesliga. Even as a young player, Beckenbauer had a very professional attitude to the way he got ready for games. He had a good understanding of the tactics of the game, too.

Beckenbauer was a runner-up in his first World Cup in 1966. He had to wait until his third World Cup before winning it. When the Netherlands got through to the 1974 World Cup Final, most football writers agreed that they were the best team in the world. But in the final, Beckenbauer marked Johan Cruijff and stopped him from playing well. Cruijff just couldn't get past Beckenbauer, and Germany were crowned World Champions.

Although Beckenbauer's main role in the team was to get back and break up attacks, he was also a fantastic dribbler, and he scored a lot of goals.

Beckenbauer had a very successful career. He won the European Cup three times, and the Bundesliga four times. He is also the only person in history to have captained and managed a World Cup winning side – he managed the West Germany team that won the 1990 World Cup.

3 Read the statements. Are they True (**T**) or False (**F**)?

1 Beckenbauer has won the FIFA World Player of the Year award.
_____

2 The sweeper position is not that popular today. _____

3 Beckenbauer won the World Cup ten years after he played his first season with Bayern Munich. _____

4 Beckenbauer didn't score many goals. _____

4 Match the phrases (1–6) with the definitions (a–f).

1 get ready	a	qualify
2 get through	b	go up one division
3 get forward	c	beat an opposition player
4 get past	d	help in defensive areas
5 get promoted	e	move towards the opposition goal
6 get back	f	prepare

Reading

1 Have you ever scored a hat-trick? What's the best hat-trick you've ever seen?

2 Read text A and complete using the prepositions below.

outside	before	for	against	on
about	for	in	at	

GREAT HAT-TRICKS

A

B

ON HIS DEBUT!

¹_____ 2004, Wayne Rooney signed ²_____ Manchester United from Everton, the club he had supported as a boy. Manchester United paid £25.6 million ³_____ him, making Rooney the most expensive teenager in world football.

United's coaching staff already knew ⁴_____ him. In fact, they remembered that he'd scored six goals for Everton ⁵_____ United in an Under-9s game, including a wonderful overhead kick.

Rooney made his debut for United in a Champions League game against Turkish side Fenerbahçe, a month ⁶_____ his 19th birthday. That night he became the youngest player ever to score a hat-trick in the Champions League. Furthermore, he scored all three goals from ⁷_____ the area. The third was a swerving free-kick.

The game finished 6-2 to Manchester United. Rooney had scored three great goals ⁸_____ his debut, and was already a hero ⁹_____ Old Trafford!

THE GREATEST OF THEM ALL?

On the last day of the 2000–01 season in Spain, Brazilian legend Rivaldo scored a **dramatic**[1] hat-trick for Barcelona against Valencia.

The quality of the goals was **incredible**[2]: a free-kick that was 30 metres from goal; another shot from a **similar**[3] distance; and then in the 89th minute, a perfect overhead kick from **the edge of the area**[4].

What really made Rivaldo a Camp Nou hero that night was the fact that Barcelona needed to win the game in order to qualify for the Champions League ahead of Valencia. Rivaldo's goal gave them a dramatic 3-2 win. Of course, with quality players like Rivaldo in the squad, managers feel there will always be **opportunities**[5] to score in games. But Rivaldo left this fantastic match-winner very late – right until the last minute of the season!

3 Read text B. Match the bold words and phrases in the text with similar meanings (1–5) below.

a exciting or thrilling

b chances

c hard to believe

d more or less the same

e just outside the box

Reading

1 Read about Pierluigi Collina's three big finals as a referee. In which game did he send off a goalkeeper?

PIERLUIGI COLLINA

The first major final that Collina refereed was the 1999 Champions League Final between Manchester United and Bayern Munich. The score after 90 minutes was 1-0 to Bayern, but as the fourth official held up the electronic board to signal three minutes of added time, United substitute Teddy Sheringham scored an equalizer. Then, as the players and fans were waiting for Collina to blow the final whistle, United scored again! Collina only gave one yellow card in the game. People remember the way he helped Bayern players to stand up after their shock defeat.

The 2002 World Cup Final is famous for being the game in which Ronaldo equalled Pelé's career World Cup goals total. The Brazilian scored his 11th and 12th World Cup goals, and Germany were unable to answer. Germany missed their midfielder Michael Ballack, who wasn't playing after getting booked in the semi-final against South Korea. The greatest thing about Collina's performance is that people don't remember it – for a referee, that's a good thing!

Collina took charge of the 2004 UEFA Cup Final between Marseille and Valencia. In the 45th minute of the game, Marseille goalkeeper Fabien Barthez brought down Valencia player Mista in the penalty area. Collina pointed to the spot and sent Barthez off. Although people remember Collina for this controversy, it was a good decision. Valencia scored the penalty, and later added a second goal. Marseille failed to score. The game is famous for Amedeo Carboni, at 39, becoming the oldest player to win a European cup final.

2 Complete the table using information in the article.

	Winners	Final score	Reason the game is remembered	Reason Collina's performance is remembered
1999 Champions League Final				
2002 World Cup Final		2-0		People don't remember it!
2004 UEFA Cup Final				

3 Read. What would you do? Tell the truth!

1 You fall in the penalty area, but you know the defender didn't touch you. What would you say to the referee?

2 You normally take the penalties for your team. In the 88th minute you feel a sharp pain in your knee. At the same time, the referee gives your team a penalty. Would you still take the penalty?

Everyday English Saying goodbye

1 ◉ 33 Listen to the two dialogues. What words and phrases are used for saying goodbye?

2 Listen again and complete the dialogues.

Dialogue 1

A: So, it's your last day today. Have you enjoyed the course?

B: Yes, it's been great. My English has improved, and I've made some good friends.

A: OK, hope to see you again. [1]_____ and good luck!

B: Thanks for everything. [2]_____!

Dialogue 2

A: [3]_____, OK?

B: Yes, let's [4]_____.

A: All right. And come and visit.

B: Cool, I [5]_____. Have a good trip!

A: Thanks, [6]_____!

Listening

1 What position is Clarence Seedorf? What trophy is he holding?

2 ◉ 34 Listen to a podcast about Clarence Seedorf. Which five clubs has he played for?

3 Listen again and answer the questions.

1 What record does Seedorf hold in the Champions League?

2 In what other competition does he hold a similar record?

3 When did he become a Legacy Champion for the Nelson Mandela Foundation?

4 What else has Seedorf done outside football?

4 Circle the correct form of the verb.

1 Clarence Seedorf *was born / has been born* in Suriname.

2 In 2007 he *became / has become* the first European to win the FIFA Club World Cup with three different teams.

3 He *won / has won* five league titles.

4 He *played / has played* in nearly 800 official club games since 1992.

5 He *scored / has scored* a great goal against Atlético Madrid in 1997.

6 He *wrote / has written* for the *New York Times*.

Pelé

Sports ambassador and professional footballer

Date of birth: 23 October, 1940

Place of birth: Três Corações, Brazil

Position: Forward

PELÉ AND THE WORLD CUP

Pelé is the only player to have won three World Cups. He made his World Cup debut in Sweden in 1958 at the age of 17. He scored a hat-trick against France in the semi-final and then two more in the final against Sweden. It was a spectacular World Cup for a 17-year-old. He is still the youngest scorer at a World Cup, as well as the youngest scorer of a hat-trick in a World Cup and the youngest scorer in a World Cup Final!

PELÉ AND HIS GOALS

Pelé scored lots of goals. He scored more than 1,200 goals in professional football, and more than 90 hat-tricks. Even though he has scored so many goals he is also famous for goals that he didn't score. In a 1970 World Cup match against England, it was his header that forced a save from Gordon Banks that many think was the greatest save of all time. And in the same competition, against Czechoslovakia, Pelé tried to chip the goalkeeper with a shot from inside his own half. It went just wide of the post.

Pelé says that his favourite goal was his 1,000th goal. It wasn't an overhead kick or a classic header – it was a penalty! But for Pelé, this meant that everybody was able to stop and watch it.

PELÉ'S FAVOURITE MOMENTS

And what two moments have given Pelé most satisfaction? His first choice is the World Cup in 1958 which was like a dream for him – a party! And his second was the World Cup in 1970 when he was an experienced player. The country of Brazil had many problems at that time. There was enormous pressure on the team, and a particular responsibility on Pelé himself – the team had to win. And they certainly did it in style. Many people feel that the goal scored by Carlos Alberto in the final against Italy was the greatest goal of all time. Pelé, of course, made the final pass.

Pelé is now an honorary ambassador for the 2014 World Cup in Brazil.

Speaking Discussion

1 Do you agree with these sentences?

1 English is important for people who work in football.

2 Being a referee is the worst job in football.

3 Compared with the players of 20 years ago, today's players are better, more skilful, and fitter.

4 Football will always be the most popular sport in the world.

Test yourself!

Check how much football vocabulary you know.
Use the clues to complete the crossword puzzle.

Across

4 I thought he had found the bottom corner but the ball hit the _____.

5 They got _____ last season so they are in the Premier League now.

7 That wasn't a penalty. The foul was outside the penalty _____.

8 I think I've _____ a muscle in my leg.

9 He isn't in the starting line-up. He's on the _____ for this game.

14 It's important for a midfielder to hold the ball and keep _____.

15 The referee thought it was a foul but I thought it was a good _____.

16 The two _____ shake hands just before kick-off.

17 The _____ has put his flag up. It's offside.

20 In 1982, Cameroon _____ for a World Cup for the first time.

22 The referee points to the spot. It's a _____.

23 He hasn't got _____ experience to be the England manager.

26 When he turns like that, he _____ me of Johan Cruijff.

27 He hit the ball hard with the outside of his boot and the ball _____ round the keeper.

29 The 2014 World Cup hosts.

30 That's a great save! He _____ the ball over the bar.

Down

1 Some people thought Michael Owen was _____ short to be a striker.

2 His ball control is excellent. He's got a great first _____.

3 Claude Makélélé is a _____ midfielder. He plays in front of the back four.

6 The winners of the first World Cup.

10 If a player kicks the ball through an opponent's legs, he _____ him.

11 Liverpool and Chelsea _____ one-all yesterday.

12 Brazilian player famous for his flip-flap.

13 The goalkeeper came out for the cross and _____ the ball comfortably.

18 Arjen Robben, Ryan Giggs and Nani are all famous _____.

19 My shoulder really hurts. I'm going to speak to the _____.

21 You should always _____ up well before the game starts.

24 How _____ do you use your left foot?

25 Their goalkeeper isn't fit at the moment. He's _____ and will be out for three weeks.

28 We can't score any goals. We really need to _____ a new striker.

Extra time!

Key:

Green: Answer the question.
Red: What or who is in the picture?
Blue: Make a question that fits the answer (more than one possible answer).
Orange: Define the word in *italics*.

Instructions for the game:

Method 1 Easy (two players)

Choose a category of question, e.g. pictures. Players A and B take it in turns to work from the top of the board to the bottom, e.g. Player A starts at square 2 and works down to square 47, Player B starts at square 6 and works down to square 43. If a player gets an answer wrong, they miss a turn. The first player to reach the bottom of the board wins.

1. HELLO. WHAT'S YOUR NAME?

2. (shin pads picture)

3. _____? "I COME FROM FRANCE."

4. WHAT IS A HAT-TRICK?

16. WHAT'S THE PAST SIMPLE OF *WIN*?

15. (goalkeeper glove picture)

14. _____? "I'M LEFT FOOTED."

13. NAME A SET-PIECE.

17. WHAT POSITION DO YOU PLAY?

18. (footballer picture)

19. _____? "I'VE LIVED HERE FOR FOUR YEARS."

20. WHAT IS A CLEAN SHEET?

32. WHAT POSITION DOES A NUMBER 9 USUALLY PLAY?

31. (scoreboard: 75:01 UNITED 2 ATLETICO 1)

30. _____? "85KG."

29. WHAT IS RELEGATION?

33. WHAT DOES CRISTIANO RONALDO LOOK LIKE?

34. (footballer picture)

35. _____? "CHICHARITO."

36. WHAT IS A SCOUT?

40. WHAT DOES A WINGER DO?

47. (whistle picture)

43. _____? "AFTER A FOUL IN THE PENALTY AREA."

44. WHO WEARS THE ARMBAND?

Method 2 Medium (two or more players)

Choose a row of questions per player. Players take it in turns to work across the board to the other side, e.g. Player A starts at square 9, Player B starts at 25, and Player C starts at 41. If a player gets an answer wrong, they miss a turn. The first player to reach the other side of the board wins.

Method 3 Difficult (two or more players)

Each player will need a coin for this method. Start at square 1. Flip a coin: heads = move forward one square; tails = move forward two squares. Players take it in turns to move through all the squares from 1 to 48. If a player gets an answer wrong, they miss a turn. The first player to reach square 48 is the winner.

5 WHAT DATE IS YOUR BIRTHDAY?

6 CAPTAIN

7 _____? "I SUPPORT ARSENAL."

8 WHAT IS A NUTMEG?

12 WHAT ARE YOU DOING TOMORROW?

11

10 _____? "LIONEL MESSI WAS BORN IN ARGENTINA."

9 WHAT IS A SKIPPER?

21 WHAT'S THE PAST SIMPLE OF *DRAW*?

22

23 _____? "I'M MAKING A CUP OF COFFEE."

24 WHAT IS ZONAL MARKING?

28 WHAT'S THE OPPOSITE OF *FAST*?

27

26 _____? "FC BARCELONA."

25 WHAT IS SQUAD ROTATION?

37 WHAT'S THE PAST SIMPLE OF *LOSE*?

38

39 _____? "I'M GOOD AT MARKING AND TACKLING."

40 WHAT IS NARROWING THE ANGLES?

44 WHO IS YOUR FAVOURITE PLAYER?

43

42 _____? "PELÉ SCORED MORE THAN 1200 GOALS."

41 WHAT IS A TRANSFER FEE?

73

Tests

UNIT 1

1 Complete the sentences using the words below.

goalkeeper ~~manager~~ central defender
midfielder winger striker

1 Josep Guardiola is a top _manager_ .

2 Karim Benzema is a _____.

3 John Terry is a _____.

4 Nani is a right _____.

5 Gianluigi Buffon is an Italian _____.

6 Steven Gerrard is a _____.

2 Read the player profile and complete Adrien's description using the words below.

> **PLAYER PROFILE**
> **Name:** Adrien Tourel
> **Nationality:** French
> **Position:** Striker
> **Favourite teams:**
>   FC Barcelona, Manchester United
> **Favourite player:** Andrés Iniesta

aren't he's they're ~~is~~ isn't I'm

"My name ¹_____is_____ Adrien Tourel.
²_____ from France, but my favourite teams ³_____ French. I like FC Barcelona and Manchester United. I think ⁴_____ the best teams in Europe.

I'm a striker, but my favourite player ⁵_____ a striker either. It's Andrés Iniesta, he is a central midfielder. ⁶_____ a fantastic player."

3 Match the words (1–6) with the words (a–f) to make football terms.

1 left-	a back
2 corner	b area
3 hat-	c flag
4 penalty	d circle
5 centre	e footed
6 full-	f trick

1 _e_ 2 ___ 3 ___ 4 ___ 5 ___ 6 ___

4 Mark each statement as True (**T**) or False (**F**).

1 You wear a hat on your head. _T_

2 You wear gloves on your feet. ____

3 You wear shin pads on your knees. ____

4 The team captain wears an armband. ____

5 You wear football boots on your feet. ____

5 Match the first part of the statement (1–5) with the second part (a–e) to make a complete conversation.

Bob

1 Welcome to England, Johan. I'm Bob Davis, the physio. ____

2 Please call me Bob. ____

3 Where are you from, Johan? ____

4 Are you the new defender? ____

5 Is that your father on the side-line? ____

6 This is our kitman Tony. ____

Johan

a Yes, I'm a full-back.

b How do you do.

c Yes, he's here for the weekend.

d OK, Bob.

e Switzerland.

f Pleased to meet you, Mr Davis.

UNIT 2

1 Complete the crossword puzzle.

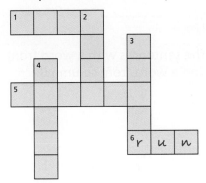

Across

1 You _____ up before training or a match.

5 When you _____ a player on the other team, you take the ball from him.

6 Can you ___*run*___ 100 metres in less than 12 seconds?

Down

2 When the other team has the ball, you _____ their players.

3 When the ball is in your penalty area, you must _____ it quickly.

4 At the start and end of the game, you shake _____ with the other team.

2 <u>Underline</u> the correct word to complete the text about a Sunday league team.

We always *play* / *plays* our matches on Sunday afternoons. We *aren't* / *don't* have training on that day. Our last training session is on Saturday morning. We *practise* / *practices* shooting and heading and the coach *name* / *names* 14 players for Sunday's game. He *don't* / *doesn't* talk tactics on Saturday. That's on Sunday, when the coach chooses the starting eleven. Sunday is my favourite day, but not if I *am not* / *don't* play!

3 <u>Underline</u> the word or phrase that doesn't go with the verbs (1–6).

1 watch …
  a game   TV   tactics

2 practise …
  set-pieces   heading   a ball

3 play …
  a five-a-side game   shooting   a match

4 have …
  pool   a day off   a favourite player

5 take …
  the gym   a free kick   a penalty

6 pass …
  forward   the ball   the team

4 Match the questions (1–6) with the answers (a–f).

1 Do you want some more vegetables? _____

2 How often do you go to the swimming pool?

_____

3 Was it a draw? _____

4 What do you think of Juventus' new away kit?

_____

5 Do you like video games? _____

6 Do you phone your parents at weekends? _____

a Probably. I know it was nil-nil about five minutes before the end.

b Usually.

c I don't mind them, but they're not my favourite.

d No, thanks.

e I hate it. Pink isn't my colour.

f Once a week.

UNIT 3

1 Match the words (1–6) with the expressions (a–f) that have similar meanings.

1 a defender	a an attacking midfielder
2 a number 10	b a forward
3 a striker	c a full-back
4 dribble	d a pass from either side
5 a foul	of the pitch into the
6 cross	opposition penalty area
	e to manoeuvre around a
	defender with the ball at
	your feet
	f an unfair act or an offence

1 _c_ 2 ___ 3 ___ 4 ___ 5 ___ 6 ___

2 Underline the correct word to complete the sentences.

Tips for young players

1 Stay *in/on/from* position at all times, and remember your team tactics.

2 Keep an eye on your team-mates. When you have the ball, look *into/around/past* you to find a free man.

3 Listen to your team-mates. If they shout "Man on!" it means there's someone in *front of/into/behind* you.

4 If you start the match *in/on/from* the bench, concentrate on the game. If you do this, you will be ready when you come *in/off/on* as a substitute.

5 If you're playing *in front of/past/in* a big crowd, don't panic. A big game can be a great experience for young players.

3 Complete the conversation using the present continuous form of the word in brackets.

A: Where's the coach?

B: He (do) _is doing_[1] an interview for the BBC.

A: Who is he (talk) _____[2] to?

B: Dan Walker.

A: Is he (take) _____[3] the training session today.

B: No. I am (do) _____[4] the training session today.

A: So when's the interview on TV?

B: It is (show) _____[5] next Saturday on "Football Focus".

4 Complete the sentences with a word from column A and a word from column B.

A	B
~~throw~~	half
additional	pass
second	time
players	offside
short	post
front	~~in~~

1 If the ball crosses the sideline and goes out of play, there's a _throw-in_.

2 The time from the 46th to the 90th minute is the _____.

3 The referee disallows the goal because there are two _____.

4 The extra minutes at the end of each half are _____.

5 The opposite of a long ball is a _____.

6 The part of the goal near the attacking player with the ball is the _____.

5 Read the conversation and put the sentences in the correct order.

a Sounds good. Why don't we buy some pizza before the game?

b No, I'm watching El Clasico.

c All right. We can go to the pizza place just near my house. They do takeaway.

d Real-Barca. Is that this evening? OK, let's watch that. Do you want to come round to my place and see it?

e OK, so see you outside the restaurant at seven?

f How about going to the cinema this evening?

1 _f_ 2 ___ 3 ___ 4 ___ 5 ___ 6 ___

UNIT 4

1 Match the words (1–6) with the words (a–f) to make football terms. Use your answers to complete the sentences.

1 back-	a kick
2 close-range	b timing
3 diving	c heel
4 good	d shot
5 overhead	e off
6 kick-	f header

1 ___ 2 ___ 3 ___ 4 ___ 5 ___ 6 _e_

1 The start of the match. _kick-off_
2 You don't use your feet and your body is horizontal for this shot. _____
3 You are near the goal when you try to score. _____
4 You pass or shoot with the ball behind you. _____
5 You always make a run at the right moment. _____
6 You jump with your feet higher than your head to try a spectacular shot at goal. _____

2 Look at the table then complete the sentences with the correct form of the verb in brackets.

African Cup of Nations 2012 Qualifying Group E							
Team	MP	W	D	L	GF	GA	Pts
Senegal	6	5	1	0	16	2	16
Cameroon	6	3	2	1	12	5	11
RD Congo	6	2	1	3	10	11	7
Mauritius	6	0	0	6	2	22	0

1 Senegal (win) _won_ the group.
2 Mauritius (not score) _____ any goals.
3 Cameroon (finish) _____ in second position.
4 RD Congo (concede) _____ 11 goals.
5 Cameroon (lose) _____ one match.
6 Two teams (draw) _____ one game.

3 Read the text and answer the questions.

George best was born in Belfast, Northern Ireland in 1946. On 14 September 1963, at the age of 17, he made his debut for Manchester United against West Bromwich Albion at Old Trafford. The game resulted in a 1-0 victory for United. His international career saw him score nine goals during 37 caps for his country. In 1974, aged 27, Best ended his time at United. He went on to play for clubs in South Africa, Australia, the USA, Ireland, England, and Scotland.

1 Where and when was George Best born?
_____

2 How old was George Best on his debut for Manchester United?
_____

3 Where did George Best make his debut for Manchester United?
_____

4 How many goals did he score during his international career?
_____

5 Name three countries George Best played in following his departure from United.
_____

4 Match the words below to find the word that describes the examples (1–6).

qualify   disallowed   score sheet
appearance   celebration   tournaments

1 You finish first in your group, you win the semi-final = you _qualify_
2 The World Cup, the Champions' League = _____
3 A player was offside, there was a foul = the goal is _____
4 You start the match; you come on as a substitute = it's an _____
5 You've scored a goal, you've won the match = It's time for a _____
6 You headed in the top right corner, you beat the keeper = you're on the _____

UNIT 5

1 Complete the commentaries (1–6) using the words below to describe the goalkeeper's actions.

~~blocks~~   punch   save   stay   narrow   tips

1 Balotelli is clear… there's only the keeper between him and the goal… but Júlio César _blocks_ the shot.

2 It's a high cross from Ribéry, but Lloris is there to _____ the ball clear.

3 Free kick. Giggs to take it. What a shot, but Casillas dives and _____ it over the bar.

4 We all thought that was a goal. But what a brilliant _____ from Petr Čech!

5 Joe Hart moves to the front post to _____ the angle, and Robben shoots wide.

6 Ali Al-Habsi didn't _____ on his line. Gerrard will have to retake the penalty.

2 Complete the sentences with the correct form of the word in bold.

1 Good goalkeepers have excellent **concentration**.
= Good goalkeepers have to _concentrate_ all the time.

2 Goalkeepers have goalkeeping coaches to **train** them in specific techniques.
= They have specific _____.

3 There has to be good **communication** between the keeper and his defenders.
= He has to _____ with his defenders.

4 A keeper needs to be able to **distribute** the ball well.
= A keeper's _____ has to be good.

5 A physio can help to **prevent** injury.
= A physio can help with injury _____.

6 A goalkeeper needs to **react** quickly.
= A goalkeeper needs quick _____.

3 Complete the text with the Past Simple or Present Perfect form of the verb in brackets.

This season (be) _has been_ [1] a good one for me. Last season I (play) _____ [2] just eight games because of a long injury, but this year I (start) _____ [3] in all our matches. I (concede) _____ [4] only six goals in ten games since September, but last season it (be) _____ [5] 15 goals in the eight games I played. It's not only me, of course: two new central defenders (arrive) _____ [6] at the club and our defence is more solid.

4 Complete the sentences with the phrases below.

pulled a muscle   broke his wrist
dislocated his shoulder   sprained my ankle
fractured the tibia   ~~bruised my shin~~

1 It really hurt when he kicked me. Luckily, I was wearing shin pads, so he only _bruised my shin_.

2 He _____ in his leg while he was warming up and couldn't come on as a substitute.

3 I turned badly on one foot and _____.

4 He _____ in his left leg in a bad tackle. He'll be out for five months.

5 He dived to make a save but his hand hit the post and he _____. Bad news for a goalkeeper!

6 He fell badly doing an overhead kick and _____. The physio had to put it back in place.

5 Match the sentences (1–6) with the responses (a–f).

1 How are you getting to the match?
2 I'm playing for the reserves tomorrow.
3 Can I give you a lift to the airport?
4 What's up?
5 Can someone give me a hand with the kit?
6 Have you had some physio?

a I think I've dislocated my shoulder.
b Great stuff. Well done!
c Not yet. It's too painful.
d No, it's OK thanks. My dad is taking me.
e By bus.
f Sure. What can I take?

1 _e_   2 ___   3 ___   4 ___   5 ___   6 ___

UNIT 6

1 Complete the crossword. All the words are adjectives to describe players.

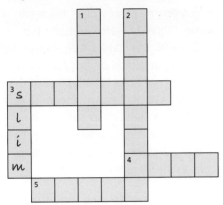

Across

3 A player who's good at dribbling and other tricks is _____.

4 If you are 192cm, you are very _____.

5 If you take risks in dangerous situations, you are _____.

Down

1 Carles Puyol has _____ hair.

2 A player who is precise in passing and shooting is _____.

3 If you eat too many hamburgers, you won't be _slim_.

2 Underline the correct word to complete the sentences.

1 Emmanuel Adebayor is _taller_ / _shorter_ than Lionel Messi.

2 Players are paid _less_ / _more_ in Finland than in England.

3 Zinedine Zidane was one of the _most_ / _least_ skilful players in the world.

4 A ticket for a Premier League game is _cheaper_ / _more expensive_ than a League 2 match.

5 Sir Alex Ferguson is _older_ / _younger_ than José Mourinho.

6 The _slowest_ / _fastest_ goal in World Cup history was scored by Hakan Şükür after 10.89 seconds.

3 Complete the coach's instructions using the words below. Some words are used twice.

should   mustn't
don't have to   ~~must~~

"If you're winning by one goal five minutes before the end, you _must_ [1] try and keep possession. You _____ [2] score another goal, but you _____ [3] concede a goal either. So your passes _____ [4] be accurate, and you _____ [5] play any long balls. If possible, you _____ [6] play a short passing game."

4 Complete the phrases with the correct form of the verb in brackets.

1 If we lose possession now the other team will (scored) _score_ .

2 If they organize their defence better they won't (conceded) _____ so many goals.

3 If we win this match we (qualified) _____ for the final.

4 He won't have so many yellow cards if he (improve) _____ his tackling.

5 He'll stay on the bench every week if he doesn't (worked) _____ harder in training.

6 They'll do well in Europe if they (signed) _____ one or two experienced players.

5 Rearrange the words to make questions.

1 match the of Who's man ?
Who's man of the match ?

2 I to improve should do What ?
_____?

3 the you about What midfielder do think new ?
_____?

4 another about goalkeeper How signing ?
_____?

5 every Do have I day weights do to ?
_____?

6 game a Why five-a-side we play don't ?
_____?

UNIT 7

1 <u>Underline</u> the word or phrase that doesn't go with the verb.

1 sign …
   a striker   <u>*a goal*</u>   *a coach*

2 give …
   advice   *a press conference*   *the match*

3 meet …
   defence   *an agent*   *the press*

4 make …
   a substitution   *a chance*   *your own luck*

5 celebrate …
   promotion   *a goal*   *relegation*

6 keep …
   going   *the target*   *the ball on the ground*

2 Complete the manager's instructions to his substitute with these prepositions.

up	away	back
~~on~~	forward	behind

"OK Hatem, our right-back's injured. I'm going to bring you <u>on</u> [1]. You've got about thirty seconds to warm _____ [2]".

"Right, you're coming on. You can go _____ [3] but remember to get _____ [4] into position as soon as we lose possession in their half. Don't let their striker get _____ [5] you, like in the last game. And don't give the ball _____ [6] – keep those passes short and simple."

3 Complete the sentences with the phrases below.

going to snow	practise set-pieces
make a substitution	play in Europe
see the physio	~~sell two players~~

1 We don't have much money. We are going to <u>sell two players</u>.

2 Our number 10 is coming off. The coach is going to _____.

3 It's painful when I kick the ball. I need to _____.

4 You're not good on corners or free-kicks, so today you will _____.

5 They say it is _____, so I'm not sure if the match will be on.

6 The team finished in fifth place, so they are going to _____ next season.

4 A European coach is describing his job. <u>Underline</u> the correct verbs.

"My job is to <u>*prepare*</u> / *make* / *play* [1] the team for each game. I *repeat* / *watch* / *return* [2] the previous match with the players, talk about what went well or badly and then *discuss* / *say* / *make* [3] tactics. I *position* / *put* / *pick* [4] the team, but the club President likes to play a part in team selection too. He's also there when I *give* / *speak* / *show* [5] the team-talk. It's the President who *does* / *makes* / *selects* [6] the big decisions, like signing players, but he listens to my ideas too."

5 Look at these comments. Are they made by a player (P) or a manager (M)?

1 That was much better this time. Well done!
   <u>M</u>

2 Not good enough, son. I'm going to take you off for the second half. ___

3 If we all continue to play well and do as the management tells us, there aren't many teams that can beat us. ___

4 You let your man get behind you. You were lucky he didn't score. ___

5 Too much talk and not enough thinking. Concentrate on your game. ___

6 It was disappointing not to score. I created a few problems for them, but it wasn't enough.
   ___

UNIT 8

1 Complete the sentences with the terms below.

~~how many~~   too much   enough time
good enough   too small   too many

1 _How many_ substitutions did the manager make?
2 Lionel Messi was once told he was _____ to play football.
3 Some people say professional footballers are paid _____ money.
4 Wayne Rooney was _____to play in the Premier League at the age of 17.
5 It's difficult to manage if there are _____ players in the first-team squad.
6 They went 1-0 down after 90 minutes and didn't have _____ to equalize.

2 Match the first part of the sentence (1–6) with the second part (a–f).

1 ~~Tall defenders often get forward…~~
2 OK, kits on, boots on…
3 Strikers need to get back and help their…
4 We lost two of our three matches and…
5 Swansea City was the first Welsh team…
6 Cristiano Ronaldo is very fast and…

a it's time to get ready.
b ~~on corners as there's a chance of a headed goal.~~
c didn't get through the group phase.
d defence when the other team is attacking.
e often gets past defenders.
f to get promoted to the Premier League.

1 _b_   2 ___   3 ___   4 ___   5 ___   6 ___

3 Complete the text with the words listed below.

~~about~~   outside   earlier
for   tie   against

How much do you know _about_[1] the early career of Gareth Bale?

On 17th April 2006, Bale played his first league game for Southampton _____[2] Millwall. At 16 years and 275 days, he was the second youngest player to appear for the club (Theo Walcott was the first a few months _____[3] in August 2005, aged 16 years and 143 days).

He signed _____[4] Spurs in May 2007. One of his first goals was a free-kick from _____[5] the area – one of his specialities.

In the League Cup home _____[6] against Middlesborough, he scored his third goal in only four starts for Tottenham.

4 <u>Underline</u> the correct verb to complete the questions.

1 How many league titles *did* / <u>*have*</u> Liverpool won?
2 What position *is* / *does* Aaron Lennon play in?
3 Why *did* / *has* Carlos Tévez leave Manchester United?
4 Where *is* / *does* Alexandro Pato playing this season?
5 What *is* / *has* Zinedine Zidane done since he stopped playing?
6 *Are* / *Do* Arsenal going to play in Europe next season?

5 Rearrange the words to make a sentence or a question.

1 trip   good   Have   a
Have a good trip .
2 here   you   course   enjoyed   Have   your
_____?
3 your   luck   future   with   career   Good
_____.
4 to   soon   you   Hope   again   see
_____.
5 by   touch   Let's   in   phone   keep
_____.
6 and   everything   thanks   Bye   for
_____.

Answer key

Unit 1

Page 6

Kick-off 1

A Wayne Rooney
B Gerard Piqué
C Iker Casillas
D Wesley Sneijder
E Dani Alves
F Franck Ribéry

Kick-off 2

1 C 2 B 3 E 4 D 5 F 6 A

Page 7

Reading 2

Age	17
Nationality	Italian
Position	Midfielder
Favourite team	Juventus
Favourite player	Marchisio

Reading 3

How old are you?
Where are you from?
What position are you?/do you play?
What's your favourite team?
Who's your favourite player?

Page 8

Vocabulary 1

a by-line
b six-yard box
c sideline
d halfway line
e centre circle
f bench
g penalty area
h corner flag

Vocabulary 3

1 d 2 e 3 b 4 a 5 c 6 f

Vocabulary 4

1 Real Madrid three, Bayern Munich nil
2 Ajax three, Shakhtar Donetsk one
3 Chelsea one, AC Milan one
4 Porto nil, Lyon two

Page 9

Reading 1

1 T 2 F 3 T 4 T 5 F
6 F 7 F 8 T 9 T 10 F

Language practice 1

2 No, it isn't.
3 No, he isn't.
4 Yes, it is.
5 Yes, he is.

Language practice 2

2 are
3 are
4 isn't
5 are
6 are

Page 10

Listening 1

1 D 2 A 3 C 4 B 5 F 6 E

Listening 2

1 c referee
2 e supporter
3 d linesman
4 a physio
5 f manager
6 b journalist

Page 11

Vocabulary 1

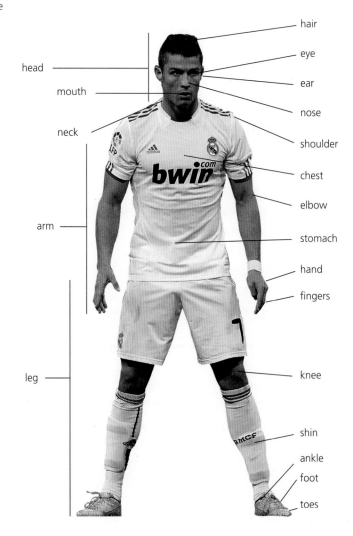

hair
eye
ear
nose
shoulder
chest
elbow
stomach
hand
fingers
knee
shin
ankle
foot
toes
head
mouth
neck
arm
leg

Page 11 (continued...)

Vocabulary 2
2 hand   4 feet   6 foot
3 arms   5 elbow

Vocabulary 3
a head   c foul   e pass
b shoot   d kick   f tackle

Page 12

Everyday English 1
1 the Academy Manager
2 the kitman
3 the manager

Everyday English 2
1 Welcome
2 Pleased to meet you
3 are you from
4 I'm from
5 Well done
6 this is
7 How do you do.

Everyday English 4
1 j   2 a   3 c   4 d   5 e
6 b   7 f   8 i   9 g   10 h

Everyday English 5
2 They're blue.
3 They're orange and white.
4 It's blue.
5 They're blue.
6 They're yellow and black.

Unit 2

Page 14

Kick-off 2
A Nemanja Vidić   central defender
B Patrice Evra   full-back
C Fabio Cannavaro   central defender
D Vincent Kompany   central defender
E Maicon   full-back
F John Terry   central defender

Kick-off 3
1 c   2 b   3 d   4 f   5 a   6 e

Page 15

Reading 3
1 centre half
2 He relaxes by listening to music and then warms up.

3 He shouts 'Clear it!' when the ball is in the penalty area. He shouts 'Mark up!' before a corner or free-kick.
4 He shakes hands with the referee and the opposition players.

Language practice 1
2 wear   6 work
3 speak   7 doesn't give
4 don't have   8 don't like
5 likes

Page 16

Listening 1
1 a   2 f   3 e   4 d   5 b   6 c

Listening 3
Tuesday
Saturday
Wednesday
Sunday
Thursday
Monday
Friday

Page 17

Reading 1
Teams get three points for a win and one point for a draw.

Reading 3
1 T   2 F   3 F   4 F

Language practice 1
2 always   4 often
3 usually   5 sometimes

Page 18

Vocabulary 1
1 D   2 A   3 E   4 B   5 C

Listening 2
1 a   2 e   3 d   4 c   5 h
6 g   7 b   8 f   9 i

Page 19

Listening 1
1 d   2 a   3 c   4 b

Listening 2
Goal 1
1 tackles
2 wins
3 gives
4 scores

Goal 2
1 passes
2 runs
3 shoots

Reading 1
A d blocks the shot
   a pass the ball to the right-back
   c shoots from outside the penalty area
   b runs forward

B d clears the ball
   b jumps
   a takes the corner
   c heads the ball

Page 20

Everyday English 1
1 Two team-mates are discussing new kit.
2 Two team-mates are talking about food likes and dislikes.
3 Two team-mates are talking about the training session.

Everyday English 2
1 Do you like   5 I can't stand
2 It's OK   6 love to attack
3 I don't like   7 hates it
4 I like   8 doesn't mind

Unit 3

Page 22

Kick-off 2
A 4-2-3-1 formation
B 4-4-2 formation
C 4-3-3 formation

Kick-off 3
A Amir   B Michael   C Robbie

Kick-off 3
Jack Wilshere – central midfielder
Nani – winger
Michael Essien – defensive midfielder
Andrés Iniesta – attacking midfielder

Page 23

Reading 3
1 Xavi Hernández
2 Ryan Giggs
3 Zinedine Zidane
4 Claude Makélélé
5 Xavi Hernández
6 Zinedine Zidane

Page 24

Reading 3
1 because it relates to the player's role within the team rather than the number on his shirt
2 no
3 no

4 in front of the midfielders and behind the strikers

5 no

6 he finds space on the pitch and helps to create chances

7 Juan Riquelme

Reading 4

2 past **4** in **6** into

3 behind **5** in front of **7** on

Page 25

Listening 1

Nationality: Spanish

Age: 17

Favourite player: Xavi

Likes: video games and listening to music

Dislikes: training with weights

Listening 2

1 T **2** F **3** F **4** T **5** F

Page 26

Reading 1

1 b **2** e **3** d **4** c **5** f **6** a

Language practice 1

2 are playing **5** are doing

3 is running **6** is looking

4 are you training

Language practice 2

Sentences to include the following phrases:

2 I'm (not) sitting

3 It's (not) raining

4 We're / We aren't / We're not working in the gym.

5 I'm (not) sending a text message.

6 My friends are / aren't playing video games.

Page 27

Vocabulary 1

1 f **2** b **3** e **4** a **5** d **6** c

Listening 1

Ken-zhi

Listening 2

2 Ken-zhi **5** Dragoslav

3 Ken-zhi **6** Ken-zhi

4 Dragoslav

Listening 3

2 a **3** b **4** c **5** f **6** d

Page 28

Everyday English 1

1 go shopping

2 watch a match on TV

3 practise for an interview

Everyday English 2

1 How about **6** sounds good

2 Let's **7** Sure

3 Why don't we **8** Let's

4 Do you want to **9** See you

5 All right

Unit 4

Page 30

Kick-off 2

1 E **2** C **3** D **4** F **5** A **6** B

Page 31

Reading 1

Spain	Italy	USA
Italy	Germany	Brazil
0	4	1
1st round	quarter-finals	1st round

Reading 2

1 disallowed **4** scoresheet

2 qualify **5** celebrations

3 appearance **6** tournament

Page 32

Language practice 1

played, needed, scored, disallowed, didn't qualify, made, were, won

Irregular verbs: didn't get, made, were, won

Language practice 2

2 scored **5** was **7** received

3 helped **6** had **8** shot

4 ran

Language practice 3

2 helped **5** received **7** ran

3 scored **6** turned **8** shot

4 was

Language practice 4

1 played **3** scored **5** won

2 lost **4** drew **6** conceded

Page 33

Listening 1

Di Stefano never played in a World Cup.

Pelé won the World Cup three times.

Pelé played for two clubs – Santos and New York Cosmos.

Maradona scored 34 goals for Argentina.

Maradona wore the number 10 shirt.

Cruyff made his Ajax debut on 15 November, 1964.

Cruyff managed Ajax, Barcelona, the Netherlands and Catalonia.

Listening 2

Refer to transcript, page 90.

Listening 3

1 e **2** c **3** a **4** b **5** a

Page 34

Pronunciation 3

liked	timed	wanted
passed	dribbled	distributed
looked	followed	
	played	
	moved	

Listening 2

1 T **2** F **3** T **4** T **5** F **6** T

Page 35

Language practice 1

2 Who **5** Where

3 Why **6** Who

4 What

Pronunciation 2

2 Did <u>you</u> think that your <u>size</u> was a <u>problem</u>?

3 Which <u>strikers</u> did you <u>like</u> when you were <u>younger</u>?

4 Were <u>you</u> a <u>goalkeeper</u> once?

5 <u>Why</u> did you <u>stop</u> playing in <u>goal</u>?

Listening 2

1 Lionel Andrés Messi

2 24 June, 1987

3 1.69 metres

4 Forward

5 Barcelona

6 53 goals in 53 appearances (2010–11)

Listening 3

2 What's his nickname?

3 When was he born? / What's his date of birth?

4 Where was he born?

5 How tall is he?

6 What position does he play? / What's his position?

7 Where did he start his career? / What was his first club? / What was the first club he played for?
8 What is his record number of goals in a season?

Page 36

Everyday English 1

1 apologizes for being late
   reason: the minibus was late picking him up
2 apologizes for playing like he's half asleep
   reason: he's really tired / he couldn't sleep last night
3 apologizes for not passing to his team-mate
   reason: he thought he had a chance to score

Everyday English 2

1 Sorry I'm late
2 did you
3 I'm sorry
4 couldn't sleep
5 What happened
6 about that
7 I'm really sorry

Unit 5

Page 38

Kick-off 2

1 E 2 F 3 A 4 B 5 D 6 C

Page 39

Reading 3

1 He plays a lot of football himself.
2 He watched DVDs of top-class keepers and spoke to some keepers.
3 The fans boo him.
4 You can upload ten different phrases for each player in the game to say.
5 Danny is very pleased with the variety of the keeper's distribution.

Reading 4

1 b 2 d 3 c 4 e 5 a

Page 40

Listening 2

1 Gym work.
2 It's his opportunity to show the manager what he can do.
3 Because he's honest with him.
4 He helped him to be professional, on and off the pitch.
5 Because it's not good for keepers to eat too many carbohydrates.
6 When he was recovering from a shoulder injury.

Listening 2

2 What are your team-mates like?
3 What is your diet like?
4 What are your days off like?

Listening 4

1 c 2 d 3 a 4 b

Language practice 1

1 made
2 do
3 made
4 doing
5 make

Page 41

Reading 2

1 T 2 T 3 T 4 F 5 F

Page 42

Language practice 1

2 have scored
3 have won
4 haven't finished

Language practice 2

2 have supported
3 had
4 made

Listening 1

Santiago Cańizares

Listening 2

German	Spanish	Czech
1956	2002	2006
neck	foot	head

Listening 3

2 muscle
3 torn
4 shoulder / ankle / wrist
5 ankle / wrist / shoulder
6 broken

Page 43

Reading 2

1 They have too many good goalkeepers to choose from.
2 David de Gea and Pepe Reina.
3 David de Gea.
4 positioning, commanding the penalty area, organizing the defence, distribution, stopping shots

Reading 3

a 4 b 2 c 1 d 3

Language practice 1

1 since   3 for
2 since   4 since

Page 44

Everyday English 1

1 take Karsten to the airport
2 give Karsten some painkillers
3 carry equipment outside

Everyday English 2

1 in the squad
2 Can I give you
3 let me
4 What's up
5 I'll have a look
6 Have you had
7 give you a hand
8 Do me a favour

Unit 6

Page 46

Kick-off 1

1 C Edinson Cavani
2 D Clarence Seedorf
3 B Emmanuel Adebayor
4 A Bastian Schweinsteiger

Kick-off 2

1 b 2 e 3 a 4 c 5 d

Kick-off 3

1 c 2 a 3 e 4 d 5 b

Kick-off 4

What's Carles Puyol like?	What does Carles Puyol look like?
He's a good leader. He's brave.	He's medium height. He's stocky. He's got long, curly hair.

Page 47

Reading 1

1 Roger Milla
2 Wembley Stadium
3 Cristiano Ronaldo
4 Manchester City
5 Brazil
6 Nottingham Forest

Language practice 1

1 older than
2 more expensive than
3 faster than
4 the fastest

Language practice 2

Sentences could include the following phrases:
taller / shorter / tougher / faster than
the tallest / shortest / toughest / fastest
more / less skilful than / the most skilful
more / less athletic than /
the most athletic

Page 48

Listening 1

The saying is a pun on George Best's name / the superlative 'best'.

Listening 2

12	5	15
not to waste the club's money	to discover good players before the big clubs	to write everything down
positive mentality	pace	goal-scoring ability
£10m	£6,000	none
when I didn't sign a bad player	when a player made his England debut	when we won the Cup

Listening 3

1 remind
2 remember
3 remind
4 remember

Page 49

Reading 1

1 E 2 C 3 B 4 A 5 F 6 D

Reading 2

1 d 2 c 3 e 4 a 5 b 6 f

Page 50

Language practice 1

2 don't have to
3 have to
4 should
5 mustn't
6 should
7 mustn't

Language practice 2

1 D – had to
2 E – should
3 A – have to
4 C – shouldn't
5 B – mustn't

Page 51

Listening 2

1 midfielder
2 He'll give them more options by scoring and creating goals.
3 He'll have to sell two of his current players and help the family move to England.

Language 1 practice 1

1 will score
2 will give
3 won't have

Language 2 practice 1

1 eat
2 lose
3 will have
4 will play

Page 52

Everyday English 1

1 advice on improving as a player
2 advice on whether to sign a player
3 advice on playing in front of scouts

Everyday English 2

1 should
2 need
3 What do you reckon
4 you mustn't
5 What do you think
6 Why don't we
7 Any tips
8 It's best if

Unit 7

Page 54

Kick-off 2

1 B 2 A 3 D 4 F 5 E 6 C

Page 55

Listening 1

1 D 2 B 3 A 4 C

Listening 2

left wing	Use the space behind him.
striker	Hit the target!
centre-back	Talk to me.
central midfield	Keep the ball on the ground.
substitute	Be ready!

Language practice 1

1 Give it to him
2 Now get back into position
3 don't give the ball away
4 Keep going
5 Shoot

Language practice 2

1 c 2 a 3 e 4 b 5 d

Page 56

Reading 3

✔	✔
✔	✔
✔	✔
✗	✔
✗	✔
✔	✗

Page 57

Listening 2

Possible answers include buying and selling players, changing formation, rotating the squad.

Listening 3

1 T 2 F 3 T 4 F 5 T

Language practice 1

1 sign 2 give 3 watch 4 speak

Language practice 2

1 going to speak
2 going to win
3 going to save
4 going to be
5 going to celebrate

Page 58

Reading 2

1 bend 2 chip 3 lob 4 curl

Page 59

Reading 3

1 b 2 d 3 a 4 c

Reading 4

1 F 2 T 3 F 4 T

Reading 5

1 no
2 He told him that he had coached at the top level.
3 They were surprised at the number of questions.
4 poorly planned training sessions and lack of attention to detail, or if the other keepers are not focused / not working to a high enough standard

Page 60

Everyday English 1

1 The manager is criticizing Karl for not scoring.
2 The manager is telling Karl to eat less pasta and bread.
3 The manager is praising Karl for playing well and scoring goals.

Everyday English 2

1 good enough
2 very few
3 as many chances as
4 How many
5 seen enough
6 How much
7 How much
8 a bit
9 too heavy
10 is enough
11 far bigger
12 Much better
13 a little lucky
14 too fast
15 a bit more
16 a few problems
17 How many

Unit 8

Page 62

Kick-off 3

1 Cristiano Ronaldo
2 Diego Maradona
3 Fabio Cannavaro

(The other players pictured are Rio Ferdinand and Lionel Messi)

Page 63

Reading 3

1 shoe salesman
2 to the Final
3 Dutch

Page 64

Language practice 1

1 too
2 enough
3 too much
4 much
5 too many

Listening 1

Lionel Messi

Listening 2

Frank
- Germany
- Brazil 1970
- Lionel Messi
- George Best
- Wayne Rooney v. Manchester City

Beatriz
- Real Madrid
- Spain 2010
- Cristiano Ronaldo
- Zinedine Zidane
- Clarence Seedorf v. Atlético Madrid

Marco
- Manchester City
- AC Milan 1989
- David Silva
- Pelé
- Marco van Basten v. Russia

Cristina
- Barcelona
- Ajax 1971
- Lionel Messi
- Johan Cruyff
- Diego Maradona v. England

Page 65

Reading 2

Beckenbauer is the only person in history to have captained and managed a World Cup-winning side.

Reading 3

1 F 2 T 3 T 4 F

Reading 4

1 f 2 a 3 e 4 c 5 b 6 d

Page 66

Reading 2

1 in
2 for
3 for
4 about
5 against
6 before
7 outside
8 on
9 at

Reading 3

1 a 2 c 3 d 4 e 5 b

Page 67

Reading 1

2004 UEFA Cup Final

Reading 2

1999 Champions League Final
- Manchester United • 2–1
- United scored two goals in injury time.
- He helped Bayern players to get up.

2002 World Cup Final
- Brazil • 2–0
- Ronaldo equalled Pelé's total of 12 career World Cup goals.
- People don't remember it!

2004 UEFA Cup Final
- Valencia • 2–0
- Amedeo Carboni became the oldest player to win a European cup final.
- He sent off Fabien Barthez and awarded a penalty..

Page 68

Everyday English 1

Goodbye, bye, see you soon

Everyday English 2

1 Goodbye
2 Bye
3 I'll text you
4 keep in touch
5 look forward to it
6 see you soon

Listening 1

midfielder; Champions League trophy

Listening 2

Ajax, Sampdoria, Real Madrid, Inter and Milan

Listening 3

1 He is the only player to win it four times with three different clubs.
2 FIFA Club World Cup
3 2009
4 He has worked on TV for the BBC; he has written a blog for the *New York Times*; he is part-owner of Monza football club, a motor-cross team, and an Asian restaurant in Milan.

Listening 4

1 was born
2 became
3 has won
4 has played
5 scored
6 has written

Crossword

Across

4 post
5 promoted
7 area
8 pulled
9 bench
14 possession
15 tackle
16 captains
17 linesman
20 qualified
22 penalty
23 enough
26 reminds
27 bent
29 Brazil
30 tipped

Down

1 too
2 touch
3 defensive
6 Uruguay
10 nutmegs
11 drew
12 Ronaldinho
13 collected
18 wingers
19 physio
21 warm
24 often
25 injured
28 sign

Extra Time!

1 *Hi, I'm X. / Hello, my name's X.*
2 a shinpad
3 *Where are you from? Where do you come from?*
4 A **hat-trick** is three goals scored by the same player in a single match.
5 (e.g.) *My birthday is on 22nd of August.*
6 an armband
7 *Which team do you support?*
8 A **nutmeg** is a technique in which a player rolls the ball through his opponent's legs.
9 won
10 gloves
11 *Which foot do you use?*
12 (e.g.) free kick, corner, throw in
13 (e.g.) *I'm going shopping tomorrow.*
14 boots
15 *Where was Lionel Messi born?*
16 **Skipper** is another word for team captain.
17 (e.g.) *I'm a central defender.*
18 bench
19 *How long have you lived here?*
20 A **clean sheet** is where the goalkeeper/team has not let in any goals during the entire match.
21 *drew*
22 corner flag
23 *What are you doing now?*
24 **Zonal marking** is a defensive strategy where defenders cover areas of the pitch rather than marking individual players.
25 A number 9 would usually play as a striker.
26 scoreboard
27 *How much do you weigh?*
28 **Relegation** is when a team is sent down to a lower division.
29 slow
31 (e.g.) *Who do you think will the Champions League this year? Who does Lionel Messi play for? Which team plays at Camp Nou?*
32 **Squad rotation** is a system of resting players and giving all players an opportunity to play.
33 (e.g.) *He's medium height. He has dark curly hair. He's athletic.*
34 diving header
35 *What is Javier Hernandez's nickname? Which footballer's nickname means little pea? Name a Manchester Utd striker.*
36 A **scout** works for a football club and looks for talented new players.
37 *lost*
38 red card
39 *What are you good at?*
40 **Narrowing the angles** is when the goalkeeper comes out towards an attacking player, making it more difficult for him to score.
41 A winger crosses, dribbles and shoots.
42 whistle
43 *When does the referee give a penalty?*
44 The team captain.
45 (e.g.) *My favourite player is Jack Wilshere.*
46 FIFA World Cup Trophy
47 How many goals did Pele score in his career?
48 A **transfer fee** is the money a club gets when it sells a player to another club.

Unit 1 Test

1

1 manager   4 winger
2 striker   5 goalkeeper
3 central defender   6 midfielder

2

1 is   3 aren't   5 isn't
2 I'm   4 they're 6 He's

3

1 e 2 c 3 f 4 b 5 d 6 a

4

1 T 2 F 3 F 4 T 5 T

5

1 f 2 d 3 e 4 a 5 c 6 b

Unit 2 Test

1

Across	Down
1 warm	2 mark
5 tackle	3 clear
6 run	4 hands

2

1 play   3 practise 5 doesn't
2 don't   4 names   6 don't

3

1 tactics 3 shooting 5 the gym
2 a ball   4 pool   6 the team

4

1 d 2 f 3 a 4 e 5 c 6 b

Unit 3 Test

1

1 c 2 a 3 b 4 e 5 f 6 d

2

1 in   3 behind   5 in front of
2 around 4 on

3

1 doing   4 doing
2 talking   5 showing
3 taking

4

1 throw-in   4 additional time
2 second half   5 short pass
3 players offside 6 front post

5

1 f 2 b 3 d 4 a 5 c 6 e

Unit 4 Test

1

1 c 2 d 3 f 4 a 5 b 6 e

1 kick-off   4 back-heel
2 diving header   5 good timing
3 close-range shot 6 overhead kick

2

1 won   4 conceded
2 didn't score 5 lost
3 finished   6 drew

3

1 George Best was born in Belfast, Northern Ireland in 1946.
2 He was 17.
3 His debut for Manchester United was at Old Trafford.
4 He scored 9 goals during his international career.
5 He played in South Africa, Australia, the USA, Ireland, England, and Scotland.

4

1 qualify   4 appearance
2 tournaments 5 celebrations
3 disallowed   6 score sheet

Unit 5 Test

1

1 blocks 3 tips   5 narrow
2 punch   4 save   6 stay

2

1 concentrate 4 distribution
2 training   5 prevention
3 communicate 6 reactions

3

1 has been	4 have conceded
2 played	5 was
3 have started	6 have arrived

4

1 bruised my shin
2 pulled a muscle
3 sprained my ankle
4 fractured the tibia
5 broke his wrist
6 dislocated his shoulder

5

1 e 2 b 3 d 4 a 5 f 6 c

Unit 6 Test

1

Across	Down
3 skilful	1 curly
4 tall	2 accurate
5 brave	3 slim

2

1 taller	5 older
2 less	4 more expensive
3 most	6 fastest

3

1 must	4 must
2 don't have to	5 mustn't
3 mustn't	6 should

4

1 score	4 improves
2 concede	5 work
3 qualify	6 sign

5

1 Who's man of the match?
2 What should I do to improve?
3 What do you think about the new midfielder?
4 How about signing another goalkeeper?
5 Do I have to do weights every day?
6 Why don't we play a five-a-side game?

Unit 7 Test

1

1 a goal	3 defence	5 relegation
2 the match	4 a chance	6 the target

2

1 on	3 forward	5 behind
2 up	4 back	6 away

3

1 sell two players
2 make a substitution
3 see the physio
4 practise set-pieces
5 going to snow
6 play in Europe

4

1 prepare	3 discuss	5 give
2 watch	4 pick	6 makes

5

1 M 2 M 3 P 4 M 5 M 6 P

Unit 8 Test

1

1 How many	4 good enough
2 too small	5 too many
3 too much	6 enough time

2

1 b 2 a 3 d 4 c 5 f 6 e

3

1 about	3 earlier	5 outside
2 against	4 for	6 tie

4

1 have	3 did	5 has
2 does	4 is	6 Are

5

1 Have a good trip.
2 Have you enjoyed your course here?
3 Good luck with your future career.
4 Hope to see you again soon.
5 Let's keep in touch by phone.
6 Bye and thanks for everything.

Transcripts

Unit 1 ⊚ 03

1 Real Madrid three, Bayern Munich nil
2 Ajax three, Shakhtar Donetsk one
3 Chelsea one, AC Milan one
4 Porto nil, Lyon two

Unit 1 ⊚ 04

1 I'm Tadame. I'm from Japan. I'm a referee.
2 I'm Marc. I'm from France. I'm a supporter.
3 I'm Hassan. I'm from Turkey. I'm a linesman.
4 I'm Marta. I'm from Spain. I'm a physio.
5 I'm Dirk. I'm from Germany. I'm a manager.
6 I'm Fatima. I'm from Egypt. I'm a journalist.

Unit 1 ⊚ 05

HT = Harry Turner, C = Conor,
M = Manager, BF = Bolaji's father

1 A Bolaji, come and meet Mr Turner.
   HT Hi, I'm the Academy Manager – Harry Turner. Welcome to England, Bolaji!
   B Thank you. Pleased to meet you, Mr Turner!
   HT Call me Harry.
   B OK, Harry!

2 C Hi, are you the new striker?
   B No, I'm a defender.
   C I'm Conor, the kitman.
   B Bolaji!
   C Where are you from, Bolaji?
   B I'm from Nigeria. Where are you from?
   C Ireland. Here you son: shirt, shorts, two pairs of socks …

3 M Well done, Bolaji!
   B Thanks, Gaffer!
   M Who's that, son?
   B Oh, this is my father, Boss.
   M Hi, pleased to meet you.
   BF How do you do.

Unit 2 ⊚ 06

On Mondays we go to the gym in the morning. At the moment, I am fast but I'm not strong. In the afternoon, we play a match.
On Tuesdays we run a lot and then we practise set-pieces. Then we play a short game on the indoor pitch.
On Wednesdays we prepare for the weekend match. We train in the morning and then, after lunch, we watch a video of our opponents. The coach speaks to us about the other team.
On Thursday mornings the strikers and midfielders practise shooting, while the defenders practise heading the ball. After lunch, everybody goes in the swimming pool.
On Friday mornings we play a five-a-side game. After lunch the manager names the team for Saturday's game. I am always in the starting 11!
On Saturdays the manager talks about tactics before the match and then it's the game!
On Sundays we have a day off. I get up at 11 o'clock. Then I play pool with my friends or play video games. In the evening I watch football on TV.

Unit 2 ⊚ 07

1 It goes in the top left corner, and that's a perfect penalty …
2 Oh, and it goes over the crossbar …
3 What a great penalty! It goes in the bottom left corner!
4 It goes wide, and he can't believe it!
5 It goes in the top right corner, and that's a wonderful …
6 And it goes straight down the middle.
7 It hits the post, and how unlucky is that?
8 Incredible; it hits the crossbar!
9 Fantastic; it goes in the bottom right corner …

Unit 2 ⊚ 08

1 Croatia have the ball. But Thuram tackles the Croatian defender and – Thuram wins the ball! The ball goes to Djorkaeff who gives it back to Thuram. Lilian Thuram is inside the penalty area now, and, it's a goal! Lilian Thuram scores for France. This is his first international goal and the score is now one-all.
2 Zinedine Zidane has the ball. Now Zidane passes the ball to Lilian Thuram. Thuram is in the right-back position. Thuram runs forward and passes to a French player. Thuram continues his run. Thuram has the ball again. Thuram shoots from outside the area. It's a goal! Now Lilian Thuram has two international goals and they are two very important goals!

Unit 2 ⊚ 09

1 A Do you like the new kit, Jérémie?
   J It's OK.
   A It's great! It's like the Milan kit.
   J Exactly. I prefer Inter. I don't like those colours!
2 B Jérémie, do you want some more potatoes?
   J Yes please. I like vegetables.
   B I can't stand them. Here, have mine!
3 C Jérémie, it's defenders against strikers in training today.
   J Fantastic. I love to attack!
   C I know, but the boss hates it when you go forward in a real game.
   J Well, he doesn't mind when I score!

Unit 3 ⊚ 10

Hi, I'm Paco. I come from Ávila in Spain, but at the moment I'm playing at an academy in England. I'm 17 years old.
My position is centre midfield like my favourite player Xavi, but in England I am playing more as a winger.
In Spain I always train with the ball, but here I'm working on fitness. I'm going to the gym a lot because I'm not very strong. But I don't really like training with weights!

In Spain I don't usually defend, but in England I have to. In fact, when we lose the ball during games, my coach often shouts at me! He says, 'Paco, what are you doing? Come deep! Track back!'

I don't have much free time in Spain. Sometimes I play video games or listen to music. In England I have more free time. I have lots of friends here, so I'm enjoying myself.

Unit 3 ⊙ 11

Dragoslav, I know you're right-footed, but you're playing on the left wing today. I want you to cut inside and shoot when you have the opportunity. You're playing well this season. I want the same again today, please! You're the skipper today, and you're taking the throw-ins too.

Now, Ken-zhi, you're one of the substitutes today, but you're coming on for the second half. You're playing in central midfield today. I want a better performance this week. Last week was terrible! You're good at tackling so don't foul anyone! It's important that you don't get another card. You don't want to be on the bench again next week, do you?

Unit 3 ⊙ 12

T = Teacher, J = Jordi

1 A Come on Jordi, we're getting paid on Friday. How about going shopping?
   J Again? Look, I can come with you, but I'm not buying anything.
   A OK. Let's take a taxi!
   J Taxi? Why don't we take a bus instead?

2 B So Jordi, what are you doing tonight?
   J I don't know really. Do you want to watch the Barça game?
   B All right. Come round to mine if you want. My mum won't mind.
   J Yeah, sounds good!

3 T Jordi, it's your first interview this afternoon, OK?
   J Sure, but is it in English?
   T Yes, of course it's in English! Let's prepare for it together.
   J Thanks, I need your help.
   T See you in the canteen at two o'clock!

Unit 4 ⊙ 13

I = Interviewer, JS = Josep Segura

I Who are the greatest attacking players of all time?
JS For me, there are four great attacking players in the history of football: Alfredo Di Stefano, Pelé, Johan Cruijff, and Diego Maradona.
I I'm too young to remember Di Stefano! Tell me about him.
JS I liked watching videos of Di Stefano when I was younger. Without the ball, he found space. With the ball, he beat players and he scored all types of goals: from close range; from long range; volleys; and he even scored a back-heel for Spain against Belgium in 1956.
I What about Pelé?
JS It's difficult for young people to understand how good he was. Pelé scored a hat-trick at the 1958 World Cup – aged 17! He had an incredible first touch and, most important of all, the ability to lose his man. He could move and score goals so quickly. And he timed his runs to perfection. He scored easy goals, and he scored difficult goals, like overhead kicks. Everybody wanted to play like Pelé!
I Your next choice is Johan Cruijff …
JS Cruijff was technically perfect and, as a Barcelona supporter, I watched him play every week. He was a great goal-scorer, but he also created a lot of goals. Cruijff often dribbled past five or six players and then passed the ball to a team-mate to score. Cruijff had good timing and nearly always made the right decision.
I Diego Maradona scored some amazing goals. Did you see him play at Barcelona too?
JS Yes, and I also followed his career with Napoli and Argentina. Maradona played with balance, strength and pace. He ran past defenders. Football looked easy! He also distributed the ball with great intelligence.
I What did these players have in common?
JS They were forwards but they moved around the pitch, and opposition teams didn't know how to stop them. Each of these players has a period of football history that is his forever.
I Are there any modern players who can join this group?
JS At the moment, Lionel Messi is the only player with the quality to join this group. He's so difficult to stop, and he's got incredible composure! He's so cool.

Unit 4 ⊙ 16

I = Interviewer, A = Andrew

I Andrew, you're one of the best young English strikers at the moment, and last week you signed a contract for a new club. Did you always want to be a footballer?
A Yes, it was always my dream to play football. The coaches at my old club told me that I was too short to be a successful striker. I'm not tall, but I grew a bit last year …
I Did you think that your size was a problem?
A No, I never thought about that. In the past, English clubs liked big centre forwards but football is different now. Anyway, I'm taller than many of the best strikers in the world.
I Which players are you talking about?
A Well, Carlos Tévez, Sergio Aguero and Javier Hernández for example. They came to England and showed that if you have good technique, size is not important in the Premier League.
I So technique is important for a striker … What other qualities does a striker need to have?
A Pace and movement! Neymar and Luis Suárez are two players who have great pace and movement. They are great finishers too.
I Which strikers did you like when you were younger?
A The best striker for me was Raúl. Wow – the top scorer in the history of the Champions League! But my favourite player when I was young was Gianluigi Buffon!
I Buffon the goalkeeper? [laughs] Really? Were you a goalkeeper once?
A Yes, I tried! But I became a striker when I was 12.
I Why did you stop playing in goal?
A I was too short!

Unit 4 ⊙ 19

A What's his full name?
B Lionel Andrés Messi.
A What's his nickname?
B He has three nicknames: Leo, La Pulga which means the flea, and El Mudo which means the mute. That's because he didn't use to say very much!
A What's his date of birth?
B 24 June, 1987.
A Where was he born?
B Rosario in Argentina.

A How tall is he?
B One metre and 69 centimetres.
A What position does he play?
B He's a forward.
A What was his first club?
B Newell's Old Boys of Rosario.
A What club does he currently play for?
B Barcelona.
A What's his record for goals in a season?
B In the 2011–2012 season he scored over 70 goals!

Unit 4 ⊚ 20

C = Coach, J-P = Juan Pablo,
TM = Team-mate

1 C Juan-Pablo! Glad you could make it this morning.
  J-P Sorry I'm late! The minibus was late picking me up.
  C When did you set off?
  J-P Not until 9.30.

2 C Come on, son. You're playing like you're half asleep!
  J-P I'm sorry, Boss. I'm really tired today.
  C When did you get to bed?
  J-P Ten o'clock. But I couldn't sleep.

3 TM What happened? I was completely unmarked!
  J-P Yeah, I know. Sorry about that.
  TM Why didn't you pass when I shouted?
  J-P I thought I had a chance to score. I'm really sorry, OK?

Unit 5 ⊚ 21

I = Interviewer, BA = Ben Amos

I Ben, what is your training programme like?
BA Hard! We work with weights in the gym, and we have training sessions and practice games outside. Modern football is very fast, so a good goalkeeper has to be fast too. At first, I found the work in the gym very difficult, but it's OK now. We do a lot of core strength work for injury prevention.
I Do you enjoy training?
BA Oh, definitely! Especially games with the first team, but also work on specific goalkeeping things such as low shots or high balls. Training's important because it's my big opportunity to show the manager what I can do. I always try to do my best.

I What is your goalkeeping coach like?
BA He's really professional and he helps me a lot. But he likes to make jokes too! He's very important because he plans quality training sessions. He prepares me for games and gives me advice, particularly when I make a mistake. I like him because he's honest with me.
I What are your team-mates like?
BA They're all good lads, and we get on. I've always tried to learn from the top players, especially from Edwin van der Sar when he was playing. He was so experienced, and had fantastic positioning. He really helped me to be professional, on and off the pitch.
I What is your diet like?
BA I'm quite careful about what I eat and drink. I try to eat healthy food. It's not good for keepers to eat too many carbohydrates, so I don't eat things like rice or bread for dinner. I also enjoy drinking litres and litres of water for hydration.
I What are your days off like?
BA I don't get many, but they're great! I like to do other sports to help me as a keeper. I started swimming after a shoulder injury and I discovered I really enjoy it. Table tennis is great for goalkeepers too! It helps to improve your reactions.

Unit 5 ⊚ 22

1
German goalkeeper Bert Trautman was a prisoner in the north of England during World War Two. After the war, he stayed in England and became a Manchester City legend. He helped City win the FA Cup in 1956. During the final, he injured his neck, but he stayed on the pitch and finished the game. He even went out to celebrate the victory after the match. Three days later he had an X-ray, and doctors found that Trautman had a broken bone in his neck!

2
In 2002, Santiago Cañizares was the first-choice keeper for Spain. But he missed the World Cup that year after an accident in his room at the team hotel! He dropped a bottle of aftershave and a piece of glass went into his foot, cutting through a tendon. He needed an operation. Iker Casillas went to the tournament as first-choice keeper in his place.

3
In October 2006, Petr Čech, Chelsea's goalkeeper from the Czech Republic, suffered a head injury in the first minute of a game against Reading. Petr Čech left the field and Carlo Cudicini came on. But he was also injured, and John Terry finished the game in goal. It was only later that people realized how serious Čech's injury was. He had surgery on his skull and returned in January 2008 wearing a rugby-style headguard which he has continued to wear ever since.

Unit 5 ⊚ 23

TM = Team-mate, K = Karsten,
D = Doctor, C = Coach

1 TM Hi Karsten. Where are you going?
  K The airport. I'm in the squad for the Germany Under-17s!
  TM That's the best news I've had all day! Well done!
  K Thanks!
  TM How are you getting there? Can I give you a lift?
  K I've ordered a taxi actually.
  TM Come on, let me take you.

2 D What's up, Karsten?
  K I've hurt my shoulder, Doc.
  D I'll have a look at it, OK? How did it happen exactly?
  K I fell on my shoulder when I went for a header.
  D Have you had any painkillers or physio?
  K Just some gel, but it's really painful.
  D Right, I'll give you something for it.

3 C Right lads, who's going to help me take this equipment outside?
  K I'll give you a hand, Coach!
  C I thought you were injured, Karsten.
  K I was, but I've had physio. My shoulder's fine now, so I'm fit to play!
  C Great stuff! Do me a favour – carry this!

Unit 6 ⊚ 24

1
I'm Steve and I've been a first team scout for 12 years, for one of the biggest clubs in the country. The most important thing is not to waste the club's money. I want quality. And the quality that I look for in a player is a positive mentality. There are a lot of good players, but only the ones with the right mentality can get to the

highest level. My most expensive signing cost £10 million. But my best moment was actually when I didn't sign a player! The president of the club and some of the other scouts all wanted to sign him during the last World Cup. I told them I didn't like the player. In the end, another club bought him for £28 million, but he's not playing well.

2

I'm Peter and I scout young players, normally 10- to 14-year-olds. I've been a scout for five years. I work for a small club, and we can't afford to pay a lot of money for players. So, the most important thing for me is to discover the best young players before the big clubs sign them. In fact, my most expensive signing was for £6,000. I love fast players. Pace is very important! My best moment in the job was when the first player I signed made his debut for the English national team. I've signed five players but he was the best. I remember when I first saw him. I thought, 'He reminds me of Johan Cruyff!'

3

I'm Richard. I'm a tactical scout. This means that I go to watch teams that my club will play against. I've never signed a player: that's not my job. The most important thing for me is to write everything down. It's essential to get players' names right! Above all, I look for goal-scoring ability. I've been a scout for 15 years and my best moment was when we won the Cup last year. Before the final, I told the manager that two of the opposition penalty-takers always kick it low and hard into the bottom right corner. The game went to penalties, and our keeper saved the penalties by those players.

Unit 6 ◎ 25

S = Scout, M = Manager

S I've seen this midfielder a couple of times. I think you should have a look at him, Boss. He will score ten goals a season, and create lots more. He'll give us more options.

M Do you think he'll be able to adapt to English football?

S I'm sure he will. He's a very professional young man, and he won't have any problems with the language.

M OK, but if we buy him, we'll have to sell two of our current players … that won't be easy. And we know that he's very close to his family. If they move to England, we'll have to help them.

Unit 6 ◎ 26

C = Coach, M = Manager, S = Scout

1 A So, now that I'm in the youth team, what should I do to improve as a player?

C Well, you need to understand more about your position – and make yourself as strong as the other lads.

A Do I have to do weights? What do you reckon?

C No, you mustn't do weights yet; you're still too young. I think you should do press-ups though, and work with rubber bands.

2 M What do you think about signing him?

S He's a decent player, Boss, and he's got a great first touch – but he's small, and I don't know if he'll grow much more.

M Why don't we speak to the other scouts?

S How about meeting them tomorrow?

3 C What's up, Alberto?

A There are a lot of scouts at the game today. I'm nervous! Any tips?

C You don't have to worry about that, son. Try to focus on your game. It's best if you take it easy for the first ten minutes, and then show them what you can do.

Unit 7 ◎ 27

Listen, boys! This is going to be a difficult game today but we're good enough to beat this team. They've beaten us too many times recently, so let's go out there and show them what we can do!

Kristian, you're on the left wing today. Their right-back always goes forward too much, so use the space behind him.

Tyrone, you're up front this afternoon. I think their goalkeeper is weak so I want you to shoot today when you have the opportunity and, most importantly, hit the target!

Daniel, the physio is happy with your knee, so you're playing at centre-back today. But if your knee is giving you problems during the match, talk to me.

Chakri, as usual, you're in central midfield. It's going to be very windy, so keep the ball on the ground.

Farooq, you're on the bench today. I need to give some other players a chance because they haven't played enough games recently. But I'm going to bring you on at some point in the game, so be ready!

Unit 7 ◎ 28

1 Stephen's free! Give it to him!
2 Great tackle, Paul! Now get back into position!
3 Marco, don't give the ball away!
4 That's good, Kai! Keep going!
5 Shoot! Oh, that was close. Good effort!

Unit 7 ◎ 29

Last season the club didn't have much money. This season, we've got lots of money, and this is what I'm going to do with it. Firstly, I'm going to buy some top players! We're probably going to play a more defensive formation at this level, so I'm going to spend on defenders. We're going to need a rotation system, because players can't play in every game at the top level. I'm going to spend big on our own young players too. In fact, we're going to build a bigger training pitch for the academy, and a new changing room for the lads. Last year travelling to away games was really difficult. This year, we're going to buy a nice new team bus. It's going to be great!

Unit 7 ◎ 30

People sometimes ask me how you can coach top keepers if you haven't played at that level. Well, when you're dealing with genuine goalkeeping legends like Peter Schmeichel or Edwin van der Sar, you can't pretend that you've played at their level. But with Edwin, I was able to say that I had coached at the top level. That way, there's a mutual respect.

Actually, when I asked Schmeichel, and later van der Sar, what they needed, they were amazed that I was really listening to them. Coaches often want to show what they know. They try to impress players with all kinds of exercises … but instead, I had a hundred questions for each of them!

Also, you make sure that every minute in training is planned properly and that you've paid attention to every detail. It's important that the other keepers in the session are really focused and able to work to a very high standard. If things aren't perfect, the number one'll get angry or even lose respect for the coach.

Unit 7 ⊙ 31

M = Manager, K = Karl

1 M How much pasta have you got on your plate?

K Just a bit, Boss. Why?

M Because you're too heavy, son! And you've got too much bread there! One slice is enough.

K But I'm going to have another training session this afternoon.

M I know that, but look what the keeper's eating, and he's far bigger than you!

2 M Not good enough, lad!

K But I've had very few balls to feet, Boss.

M Come on, Karl! You've had as many chances as anybody else. How many opportunities do you need before you score?

K Sorry, Boss, but they're marking me out of the game!

M Well, I've seen enough for today. I'm going to take you off for the second half. How much did we pay for you?

3 M Great work, Karl! Much better!

K Thanks, Boss! I got a little lucky for the second goal.

M You make your own luck, son. You were too fast for them.

K Am I going to play a bit more now, Boss?

M Well, you've created a few problems for their defence today, and you've got a couple of good goals. How many are you going to score for us this season?

Unit 8 ⊙ 32

1

Hi, I'm Frank, and I'm a Manchester United fan. For me, Germany are the greatest team around at the moment with players like Mesut Ozil, Mario Götze and Thomas Müller. I think the greatest team of all time has to be the Brazil team from the 1970 World Cup. Lionel Messi's the best player in the world today, but Wayne Rooney's strike against Manchester City is the greatest goal ever! The all-time greatest player is George Best.

2

Hi, my name's Beatriz, and I'm a Real Madrid fan. Here are my favourites … Current team: Real Madrid! Best team of all time? The Spanish team that won the World Cup in 2010. In terms of players, I'd say Cristiano Ronaldo's the best today, but Zinedine Zidane's the greatest ever. And the goal? I'd choose Clarence Seedorf's strike against Atlético Madrid – for Real, of course!

3

I'm Marco, and I'm a Milan supporter. But, in my opinion, the greatest current team is Manchester City. The best team of all time is the AC Milan team from 1989 – the one with the three amazing Dutch players. My favourite player at the moment is David Silva. I loved Marco van Basten, and his goal against Russia in the European Championships is the best ever! But I think the greatest player in the history of the game has to be Pelé.

4

I'm an Ajax supporter and my name's Cristina. The best team ever is the 1971 Ajax team. That really was total football! But Barça are the best team at the moment, and I think Lionel Messi's the number one player. Maybe, if he can keep going, in future we'll be able to compare him with the greatest player of all time – Johan Cruijff. The best goal I've ever seen was Diego Maradona's dribble against England.

Unit 8 ⊙ 33

T = Teacher

1 T So, it's your last day today. Have you enjoyed the course?

A Yes, it's been great. My English has improved, and I've made some good friends.

T OK, hope to see you again. Goodbye and good luck!

A Thanks for everything. Bye!

2 A I'll text you, OK?

B Yes, let's keep in touch.

A All right. And come and visit …

B Cool, I'll look forward to it. Have a good trip!

A Thanks, see you soon!

Unit 8 ⊙ 34

A Today, we're talking about Clarence Seedorf …

B Yes – one of the greatest midfielders in the history of football. He's been so consistent at the top level – not many players have won as many trophies as Clarence.

A He's made fans happy wherever he's played, and he's helped lots of people outside the sport as well, especially children.

B Clarence was born in Suriname, a former Dutch colony in South America, but he grew up in the Netherlands …

A This guy's got an amazing record! He's won five league titles in three different countries. He's played in nearly 800 games for Ajax, Sampdoria, Real Madrid, Inter and Milan …

B But it's his Champions League record that's really special, isn't it?

A Yes, in fact, he's won the competition four times, and is the only player to do this with three different clubs (Ajax in 1995, Real Madrid in 1998, and Milan in 2003 and 2007).

B He was also the first European to win the FIFA Club World Cup with three different teams (Ajax in 1995, Real Madrid in 1998, and Milan in 2007).

A And we can't forget that Clarence has scored some magnificent goals too, including a famous strike from distance against Atlético Madrid for Real.

B He's also played in three European Championships, and a World Cup with the Netherlands.

A Outside football, he's founded the Champions for Children social development programme, and in 2009, he became a Legacy Champion for the Nelson Mandela Foundation.

B That's enough, right?

A Not for Clarence! You see, he's also worked on TV for the BBC and written a blog for the *New York Times*. He's even part-owner of Monza football club, a motor-cross team, and an Asian restaurant in Milan! He's obviously an intelligent man …

B Yes, it's not surprising that people call him 'the professor' in Italy.

A–Z wordlist

A
academy /əˈkædəmi/
added/additional time /ˌædɪd, əˌdɪʃənl ˈtaɪm/
agent /ˈeɪdʒənt/
appearance /əˈpɪərəns/
armband /ˈɑːmbænd/
attack v /əˈtæk/
away game /əˈweɪ ˌgeɪm/

B
back-heel /ˈbæk ˌhiːl/
ball /bɔːl/
beat v /biːt/
bench /bentʃ/
bend v /bend/
bib /bɪb/
block v /blɒk/
boots /buːts/
boss /bɒs/
break/broken [break a bone] /breɪk, ˈbrəʊkən/
by-line /ˈbaɪ ˌlaɪn/

C
captain /ˈkæptɪn/
celebrate /ˈselɪbreɪt/
central /ˈsentrəl/
centre circle /ˈsentə ˌsɜːkl/
centre-back /ˈsentə ˌbæk/
centre-half /ˈsentə ˌhɑːf/
champions /ˈtʃæmpiənz/
Champions League /ˈtʃæmpiənz ˈliːg/
chest /tʃest/
chip v /tʃɪp/
clean sheet /ˌkliːn ˈʃiːt/
clear v /klɪə(r)/
close-range shot /ˌkləʊs ˌreɪndʒ ˈʃɒt/
club /klʌb/
coach n and v /kəʊtʃ/
commentary /ˈkɒməntri/
competition /ˌkɒmpəˈtɪʃn/

composure /kəmˈpəʊzə(r)/
concede /kənˈsiːd/
control n and v /kənˈtrəʊl/
corner /ˈkɔːnə(r)/
corner flag /ˈkɔːnə ˌflæg/
create /kriˈeɪt/
creative /kriˈeɪtɪv/
cross n and v /krɒs/
crossbar /ˈkrɒsbɑː(r)/
curl v /kɜːl/
cut inside /ˌkʌt ɪnˈsaɪd/

D
defence /dɪˈfens/
defend /dɪˈfend/
defender /dɪˈfendə(r)/
defensive /dɪˈfensɪv/
disallow /ˌdɪsəˈlaʊ/
dislocate /ˈdɪsləkeɪt/
distribute /dɪˈstrɪbjuːt/
distribution /ˌdɪstrɪˈbjuːʃn/
dive v /daɪv/
diving header /ˌdaɪvɪŋ ˈhedə(r)/
division /dɪˈvɪʒn/
draw n and v /drɔː/
dribble /ˈdrɪbl/

F
fan /fæn/
final /ˈfaɪnl/
first round /ˈfɜːst ˌraʊnd/
first touch /ˈfɜːst ˌtʌtʃ/
fit /fɪt/
five-a-side /ˈfaɪv ə ˌsaɪd/
foot/feet /fʊt, fiːt/
formation /fɔːˈmeɪʃn/
forward n /ˈfɔːwəd/
foul n and v /faʊl/
fourth official /ˌfɔːθ əˈfɪʃl/
fracture v /ˈfræktʃə(r)/
free-kick /ˌfriː ˈkɪk/
full-back /ˈfʊl ˌbæk/

G
gaffer /ˈgæfə(r)/
game /geɪm/
gloves /glʌvz/
goal /gəʊl/
goal kick /ˈgəʊl ˌkɪk/
goal line /ˈgəʊl ˌlaɪn/
goalkeeper /ˈgəʊlkiːpə(r)/
goalscorer /ˈgəʊlskɔːrə(r)/

H
half time /ˌhɑːf ˈtaɪm/
halfway line /ˌhɑːfweɪ ˌlaɪn/
hand-ball /ˌhænd ˈbɔːl/
hat-trick /ˈhæt ˌtrɪk/
head v /hed/
home game /ˈhəʊm ˌgeɪm/

I
injured /ˈɪndʒəd/

J
journalist /ˈdʒɜːnəlɪst/
jump /dʒʌmp/

K
kick v /kɪk/
kick-out /ˈkɪk ˌaʊt/
kit /kɪt/

L
league /liːg/
left-back /ˌleft ˈbæk/
left-footed /ˌleft ˈfʊtɪd/
linesman /ˈlaɪnzmən/
lob v /lɒb/
long ball /ˈlɒŋ ˌbɔːl/
long-range shot /ˌlɒŋ ˌreɪndʒ ˈʃɒt/
lose /luːz/

M
manager /ˈmænɪdʒə(r)/
mark v /mɑːk/
match /mætʃ/
medal /ˈmedl/
midfield /ˌmɪdˈfiːld/
midfielder /ˌmɪdˈfiːldə(r)/
muscle /ˈmʌsl/

N nil /nɪl/
nutmeg v /ˈnʌtmeg/

O offside /ˌɒfˈsaɪd/
onside /ˌɒnˈsaɪd/
opposition /ˌɒpəˈzɪʃn/
overhead kick /ˌəʊvəˌhed ˈkɪk/

P pace /peɪs/
pass n and v /pɑːs/
penalty /ˈpenəlti/
penalty area /ˈpenəlti ˌeəriə/
penalty spot /ˈpenəlti ˌspɒt/
penalty-taker /ˈpenəlti ˌteɪkə(r)/
physio /ˈfɪziəʊ/
pitch /pɪtʃ/
play v /pleɪ/
player /ˈpleɪə(r)/
point n /pɔɪnt/
position /pəˈzɪʃn/
possession /pəˈzeʃn/
post n /pəʊst/
press conference /ˈpres ˌkɒnfərəns/
professional /prəˈfeʃənl/
promoted /prəˈməʊtɪd/

Q qualify /ˈkwɒlɪfaɪ/
quarter-final /ˌkwɔːtə ˈfaɪnl/

R receive /rɪˈsiːv/
record n /ˈrekɔːd/
referee /ˌrefəˈriː/
reflexes /ˈriːfleksɪz/
relegated /ˈrelɪgeɪtɪd/
result /rɪˈzʌlt/
right-back /ˈraɪt ˌbæk/
right-footed /ˌraɪt ˈfʊtɪd/
run /rʌn/

S salary /ˈsæləri/
save n and v /seɪv/
score n and v /skɔː(r)/
scoresheet /ˈskɔːʃiːt/
scout /skaʊt/
season /ˈsiːzn/
semi-final /ˌsemi ˈfaɪnl/
set-pieces /ˌset ˈpiːsɪz/
shake hands /ˌʃeɪk ˈhændz/
shin pads /ˈʃɪn ˌpædz/
shirt /ʃɜːt/
shoot /ʃuːt/
shorts /ʃɔːts/
shot /ʃɒt/
side-foot v /ˈsaɪd ˌfʊt/
sideline /ˈsaɪdlaɪn/
sign v /saɪn/
six-yard box /ˌsɪks ˈjɑːd ˌbɒks/
skill /skɪl/
skipper /ˈskɪpə(r)/
slide tackle /ˈslaɪd ˌtækl/
socks /sɒks/
sprain v /spreɪn/
squad /skwɒd/
squad rotation /ˈskwɒd rəʊˌteɪʃn/
stadium /ˈsteɪdiəm/
striker /ˈstraɪkə(r)/
substitute n /ˈsʌbstɪtjuːt/
substitution /ˌsʌbstɪˈtjuːʃn/
supporter /səˈpɔːtə(r)/

T tackle n and v /ˈtækl/
team /tiːm/
team-mate /ˈtiːm ˌmeɪt/
through-ball /ˈθruː ˌbɔːl/
throw-in /ˈθrəʊ ˌɪn/
timing /ˈtaɪmɪŋ/
tournament /ˈtʊənəmənt/

train v /treɪn/
training /ˈtreɪnɪŋ/
training ground /ˈtreɪnɪŋ ˌgraʊnd/
transfer n /ˈtrænsfɜː(r)/
transfer fee /ˈtrænsfɜː ˌfiː/
trophy /ˈtrəʊfi/
turn n and v /tɜːn/

V volley n and v /ˈvɒli/

W warm up /ˌwɔːm ˈʌp/
wide /waɪd/
win /wɪn/
winger /ˈwɪŋə(r)/
winners /ˈwɪnəz/
World Cup /ˌwɜːld ˈkʌp/

Z zonal marking /ˈzəʊnl ˌmɑːkɪŋ/